Here My Home Once Stood

By Moyshe Rekhtman
With Phil Shpilberg

Fourth Generation Publishing

ISBN: 978-0-615-21703-1

First Edition Published August 20th, 2008

Website: www.heremyhomeoncestood.com

Please direct any questions or comments regarding the contents of this book to: phil@heremyhomeoncestood.com

Editing: James McDonough, Ph.D., Sandra Shpilberg, Elliott Brown, Ashley Jenkins

Book Cover Design: James Lovekin

Front Cover: All that remains of Kalyus - a monument over the mass grave of 540 Jews of Kalyus, Ukraine - erected by Moyshe Rekhtman in the 1980s

Back Cover: Letichev concentration camp (photo circa 1917 – source Wikipedia)

Proceeds from this book will be donated to the United States Holocaust Memorial Museum

Dear grandfather:

Thank you for all you have given us.
Thank you for living to see your story in print.
Without you there is nothing.

Prologue

Each of us knows him in our own intimate and vastly different way. To my mother, he was a strict father, unyielding when it came to curfews, academics, and discipline. He was a young father, lanky and impossibly thin. He loved to read and was known to lift the books others were reading and lock himself in the bathroom with them for hours. He had so many volumes a curious toddler grandchild would later ask him why he had so many copies of the same book.

To me, he is a loving grandfather and, in many ways, my best friend. He taught me to read, play chess, and ride a bike. He was the one I could always count on during a turbulent childhood. He was there for the long and confusing trek from the Soviet Union to the United States via Austria and Italy. He walked me to school long after I stopped needing an escort, turning back a few blocks short to spare an insecure high-school sophomore any undue embarrassment. That was the last year his sight allowed him to walk by himself, and he must have known it. If he did know, he made no fuss about it. He simply gave me a kiss, turned around, and walked home each day, considering himself exceedingly fortunate.

The next generation sees him much differently, and he sees it not at all. To his great-grandchildren, he is a figure only able to give love, a lot of love. He has given himself to his family for many years and now he is frail. His mind is sharp, but his eyes have been eaten away by time, illness, and hardships few can fathom. His youngest great-grandchild, my son, lives three thousand miles away from him and sees his *diedushka* only two or three times a year. Yet this aged patriarch has a profound impact on my son. There is something surreal about the way the toddler loves this hulking figure who seldom gets up from his armchair. They have a bond, as all of us do, that only an unbroken link from so far away and so long ago can explain. The tot zooms by as his great-grandfather tries to hug him, arms flailing helplessly but without panic or frustration. To the little one, it's a game. He may run past his grandfather many times but there will always be the embrace and kiss at the end. He won't do it right there and then, but my son will talk about his love for his grandfather later. Back home he will ask me to call him and greet grandpa's excited voice with the same words we all speak to him "*Ya tebia lublu, dieda*"—I love you, grandfather.

There is this Moyshe Rekhtman, weathered and sightless, loving and patient. There was the Moyshe of the long walks to school, the one who taught the letters and the chessmen's moves. There was the young Moyshe who struggled to raise two daughters in the impoverished postwar Soviet Union, the one who stayed with his youngest daughter in the crumbling USSR as the rest of the family moved to New York in the late 1970s.

But before this Moyshe Rekhtman, there was another one. There was the one who refused to die in the Nazi killing fields of the Ukraine. Everything he was, everything he is, everything we are, and everything we will become was forged in those blood-soaked years when a 14-year-old walked out of the valley of death to give us life. And whether we have known his story for many years, as I have, or are yet to learn it, as my son will, our hearts are filled with deep love, sympathy, and admiration for this great man.

Just as sight was escaping Moyshe's failing eyes, my cousin Alex asked him to tell about everything that had happened to him in those dark war years. Instead of telling his story to one grandson, he decided to tell the story to all the generations that will follow. In 1992, Moyshe felt for the record button on his tape player and recorded the contents of this book in Russian.

I first heard the story in 1995 and it moved me deeply. A few years later, I tried to translate it to English to preserve the memory of my dear grandfather. Alas, working with the noisy cassettes in a tongue growing more foreign to me by the day proved too much for me. It was only in 2003 that I could take to the task in earnest. The technology to digitize my grandfather's recording had finally arrived. It was then, ten years after my grandfather felt for the stop button, that I gathered the dictionaries and my laptop and finally willed myself to feel for the play button on my iPod. The time has come.

Phil Shpilberg, July 2007

I would like to tell of the tragic events that took place fifty years ago, to which I was a witness, and in which I played a part. I want you to know about my family and friends, and about my village, Kalyus, where I passed my short and difficult childhood. Unfortunately, I cannot take you to the place where I was born because, among other reasons, we now live very far from where I once lived. My children and grandchildren will likely never visit the soil where my family history took place. Instead I will tell you everything I remember, so that you will at least have some idea of what happened in those times. I also want you to know where you come from, and who your ancestors were. As the years pass, you will undoubtedly ponder these questions, and nobody will be there to answer them. Much time has gone by, and there are many things that I have forgotten. Yet there are many scraps of memories that remain, and I shall put them together for you.

I was born on November 15, 1927, in the village of Kalyus, Kamenets-Podolskaya Oblast[1] (currently called Khmelnitskaya Oblast). The village lay on the Dniester River, which was, at that time, the natural and political border with Romania's Bessarabia. Kalyus was far from any railroad stations or major roads, and it seemed to be forgotten by both God and man. It was flanked by mountains on one side, on the other by a pine forest. A brook flowed through the middle of the village, dividing it into two parts. On one side lived the Jewish population, and on the other the Ukrainian people. Ukrainians and Jews lived well together, knew each other by name, studied and worked together, and helped each other in their daily lives. Today, my village no longer exists. In the early 1980s, a hydroelectric station was built on the Dniester River, and the village was submerged under a reservoir. Therefore, no trace of my childhood neighborhood remains.

---

[1] The Soviet Union was divided into republics, which where further divided into oblasts.

About two hundred and fifty families lived in the village, and they were mostly poor. The adults worked either on the Jewish collective farm or in the tobacco factory. My father, Shika, and mother, Rachil, worked on the farm until 1939. When a hat factory opened, my father began working as an artisan in the hat-making trade, the craft he had learned as a young man. I was the oldest of three children. My sister, Ronya, was born in 1934, and my brother, Isaak, in 1940. I can no longer recall their faces, but I have never stopped loving them. My paternal grandparents, Iosif and Mira, were tailors who made new clothes and mended old ones for both the Jews and the Gentiles of Kalyus and the surrounding villages. They were kind, honest people and were known and liked by Jews and Gentiles alike.

My parents were simple people who earned everything they had with their own toil and sweat. They had no formal education and were illiterate. Their lives were difficult, but they persevered. My mother lost her father at age seven. Her mother, Menya, lived in Luchenets in Vinitskaya Oblast, about 50 kilometers from Kalyus, but visited us often. My mother was a gentle, kind person who was compassionate to those around her. My paternal grandparents loved her as if she were their own child. My father loved her and indeed was deeply devoted to all of his family. The loving home of my parents is omnipresent in my memories and, even now, I can see their faces and hear their voices.

To us children, Kalyus felt like heaven. We did not understand the material difficulties that our parents experienced, nor did we understand that we were living in absolute poverty. Our entertainment was simple and enjoyable. We played outside barefoot from early spring to late fall. We disappeared into the forest or swam in the river for whole days during the spring and summer. In the winter we rode homemade sleds and skis or skated over ice on improvised skates. We never refused food and ate everything that could be called edible. We were not picky about our garments and wore anything that passed for clothes. Despite how poor we were, my family lived better than most other families in the village. My grandparents' earnings were always able to buy food. Because my parents worked at the collective farm, we were allowed to keep our own garden patch and grow potatoes, corn, and vegetables for ourselves. We also owned a goat that gave fresh milk every day.

Kalyus was so secluded that most of the residents never left its limits. Even Novaya Ushitsa, the center of the region, was too distant for travel on foot. There were no cars, and the collective farm bought its first trucks only two years before the war. I was one of the lucky children who got to see the world outside the village. My grandfather brought me with him to Mogilev Podolsk, to see his daughter, Aunt Sima. Mogilev Podolsk was a big city compared to Kalyus, and when I came home I told my friends about the miracles I saw there. I spoke of eating ice cream and drinking carbonated water. I raved that there was electricity and a working radio in every home! My friends listened with envy when I told them that twenty-five kopecks bought a movie ticket on any day of the week. In Kalyus, we saw a movie every two or three months when a mobile screen and a projector came to the village.

On June 22nd, 1941, my family was eating lunch together when my grandmother burst into the house and told us that Germany had attacked. My father ran to the village council and came back looking very upset. He found out that the Germans had bombed Kiev, Odessa, and every other major city in the Ukraine during the night. Battles against the Germans were raging along the European boarder of the Soviet Union, from the Baltic Sea to the Black Sea.

War itself was not new to us. My maternal grandfather, who was my namesake, had died fighting in the First World War. When Germany attacked Poland on September 1, 1939, the Soviet Union gladly helped Germany defeat it. My father was drafted into the Soviet army and spent three months on the Polish front. That same year, on August 23—a mere nine days before Germany invaded Poland thus starting World War II– Germany and the Soviet Union had signed a nonaggression pact and secretly divided up Eastern Europe between them.

On November 30, 1939, the Soviet Union attacked Finland. The newspapers reported to be a war instigated by the Finns. (History tells something quite different.) Words of heroism and the imminent victory spilled from the pages of the Soviet papers. But this distant war had little effect on life in Kalyus. There was no draft for the Finnish war in Kalyus, and we went about our daily lives. The Finnish War ended in March 1940. Then in the spring of 1940, Soviet soldiers appeared in Kalyus. They frantically prepared for defense of the border. They were getting ready for war, and we believed it would be with Romania. However, on June 28, 1940, Romania surrendered Bessarabia, the region bordering the Ukraine across the Dniester, to the Soviet Union.

After the surrender of Bessarabia, the soldiers who had assembled the border fortification were now dismantling it. Life in Kalyus actually improved greatly when the military was there. The soldiers organized dances in the meadow on Sundays, which were well attended by the young people of the village. Likewise, the soldiers came to the farm club evenings and often brought movie projectors to show films. The influx of young men also led to better business for the locals. The tobacco farm started paying regular wages due to increased revenues. All the craftsmen working at the sewing shop, including my father, received regular wages. The farm gave out more food. A bakery and grocery store opened, providing more choices than previously available. At that turbulent time we used to say, not without irony, "Life has become better, life has become more fun."

However, by the spring of 1941, we had little doubt that something was about to happen. The defense ministry frequently called men for military training, and my father had to leave for days or weeks at a time. He told us that despite the nonaggression pact which the Soviet

Union had signed with Germany, the Soviet Union was preparing for war. Of course, the newspapers wrote that relations between the Soviet Union and Germany were excellent and that our enemies, the English and the Americans, were aiming to divide us. The Soviet Union would not succumb to such provocations, they wrote.

We had lived through the age of war, but this news on June 22, 1941, was different. Somebody had attacked the mighty Soviet Union just kilometers away from our secluded village! Our village leaders called a meeting in a few hours to explain the situation. The news quickly spread through the village, and everyone was in the center square by the time the meeting started. The head of the local Communist party, the chairman of the border patrol, and a representative of the local war command led the meeting. They told us that the Germans had mounted an unprovoked and unannounced attack on our homeland. They assured us that the war would not last long because our glorious Red Army would destroy the enemy quickly. After all, it had already proven itself in the battles with the Poles and the Finns. They further assured us that the battles would take place on enemy territory, and that we had nothing to fear. The war-command representative announced that men of fighting age were required to report to the regional ministry of war at ten o'clock in the morning on the following day. Nobody at that meeting could have predicted that the war would be so cruel, last four years, and take such a huge number of human lives.

My father and Uncle Yankel were among the draftees. My mother prepared father's backpack that same evening. She included sets of clothing, a spoon, kettle, mug, and as much bread as the sack would hold.

The next morning my father and the other draftees climbed into the horse-drawn cart provided by the collective farm. As the horses pulled them away from the village, everybody trailed them far past the village limits. Many of the villagers were crying for their loved ones, and fearing the unknown.

Uneasy days followed. We had no idea what was happening. Newspapers came many days late and were filled with propaganda, half-truths, and, as it later turned out, outright lies. The authorities insisted that the fighting would not extend further into Soviet territory than the old border with Bessarabia—right across the Dniester from Kalyus. The authorities ordered all oil lamps extinguished at night for the village to avoid becoming a bombing target. The boys too young for military service diligently attended to this order. But the sounds of artillery fire remained distant, and actual fighting never came to us, as we were far from the main roads. No military units moved through Kalyus.

A week after the initial draft, another war-command representative arrived at Kalyus and gathered all the sixteen- and seventeen-year-old boys who were just below the draft age. To the agony of their mothers, many of whom had just parted with their husbands and older sons, he told the boys to prepare quickly to travel to the region center and report to weapon-making factories.

However, these boys were not away for long. They returned a few days later, looking hungry, dirty, and very frightened. As soon as they had arrived in Vinnitsa, the city was heavily shelled by German airplanes. The war-command representative disappeared, and they were left on their own. The city was in complete chaos, and the boys had nowhere to go and decided to come home. The roads were full of retreating Red Army soldiers and fleeing civilians. German airplanes were bombing the retreat routes, and the roads became littered with human and horse bodies. In addition to the nonstop bombing, the hot weather was also tormenting the thirsty and hungry refugees. Giant lines were forming at water wells as people tried to drink and get water for their horses. Many of the wells were already dry. The young men returned to Kalyus and saved themselves from the anarchy happening outside. Had they joined the fleeing masses, perhaps they would have survived the war.

Leaving Kalyus had been a common ambition for the young people of the village. We were eager to leave in order to taste modern, urban life. A few months prior to the war, I had finished the school year, remaining on the honor roll for the seventh consecutive year. Students who finished seven years of school were eligible to enroll in a vocational college. I wanted to use this opportunity to move to a city and continue my studies there. My parents, however, were dead set against this because they believed me too young to live on my own. My teachers also agreed that I should finish ten grades, albeit for different reasons than those of my parents. I had been an outstanding student, and they believed I could enroll in a university of my choice if I completed my studies. My father was working day and night to earn enough to educate his children. I could not disobey my parents and teachers, and so I agreed to remain in Kalyus for three more years. Those that finished high school were preparing to leave for the cities. Some were entering military schools while others were going to enroll in universities. My friends and I were jealous of our classmates who were leaving because we still had years of school in Kalyus left. We could not have imagined that these were the last few peaceful days. No one was going anywhere.

The news of the chaos on the roads prevented everyone else from trying to flee. The villagers' fate was further sealed by the fact that neither the village council nor the farm gave anyone transport outside Kalyus. The nearest railroad station was sixty kilometers away, and evacuation was impossible for the common people of Kalyus. Only a few Jewish families managed to escape. The director of the tobacco factory and his family, as well as the chairman of the Jewish council and his daughter managed to find passage out of Kalyus at the last possible moment. They all survived the war by moving deep into Russia.

Soon retreating Soviet military units began appearing in Kalyus. The soldiers were ragged, dirty, and hungry. They told of brutal battles and total German military superiority. The Germans were better organized, better equipped, and were inflicting a huge number of casualties on the Red Army, which was powerless to slow the enemy's advance. After only three weeks of war, we woke up to find ourselves entirely without government. All the Communist officials had fled during the night. There would also be no more retreating units, and we were left to our own fate. It was during these days of anarchy that somebody pried open the locks of the general store and the tobacco plant. The villagers looted the stores and factories and took home whatever they could find. The store was already almost empty by this time because people had stocked up on food at the start of the war. However, the tobacco plant warehouse was full of cigars, cigarettes, and raw tobacco. I brought home a lot of tobacco products and hid them in the attic. They came in very handy later as we exchanged them with the Gentiles in Kalyus for food.

A few days later we saw the first German soldiers. About twenty large, young soldiers rode motorcycles up the bank of the Dniester. They were dressed in full military uniforms with sleeves rolled high. They wore metal helmets and carried automatic weapons slung around their necks. We had heard many rumors about Germans and their cruelty toward Jews. I heard that they abused Jews and forced them to live in ghettos in Poland. The Soviet papers had widely publicized their mistreatment of Jews before the nonaggression pact was signed. However, reporting stopped after the signing. We even heard rumors that Germans engaged in mass murder of Jews, but this was so far-fetched that most refused to believe it.

The soldiers stopped at the village well and dismounted their motorcycles to drink. They got back on and rode off toward Novaya Ushitsa without saying a word to us.

After that, a few civilians who called themselves Ukrainian nationalists appeared in Kalyus. They came from the western oblasts of the Ukraine, which had belonged to Poland before 1939. These nationals cooperated with Germany right from the beginning, and Hitler promised them an independent Ukraine in exchange for their loyalty. They were helping Germany establish Hitler's so-called new order in the newly occupied territory. Ukrainians had suffered greatly under Stalin and sought vengeance.

Before the war, our remote village seemed to be forgotten by all. But Stalin's heavy hand did not bypass it. People disappeared in the middle of the night and were never heard from again. The authorities claimed that they were spies, Zionists, and other sorts of traitors, but nobody believed these baseless accusations. These "spies" had lived in Kalyus since childhood. Besides, nobody's affairs were entirely private. But nobody dared to speak of it, even the parents in front of their own children, lest they should be next to disappear into the night.

The Communists never wasted an opportunity for some good propaganda. During the May holidays before the start of the war on June 22, the whole school went to the Dniester for a political rally. Teachers, dignitaries, and party members sang the praises of our comrade Stalin and his government for the good life and the joyful childhood that they had given us. We then danced as an orchestra played loudly. The music carried all the way to the other shore of the Dniester, where the Romanians watched with envy. They believed us to be the happiest people in the world.

Of course we were far from lucky. Besides flooding us with endless propaganda, Stalin had forced the Ukraine into an artificial, unnecessary famine in 1933. It started in the winter of 1932–1933, but I remember the spring and summer of 1933 being particularly difficult. This was a scary time because people ate anything they could find. We started with the farm animals, and then ate cats and dogs; and then, finally, everything living until no animal or insect life remained. In the spring, when leaves appeared on trees and grass on the ground, people ate those too. Whole families were dying from lack of food. The Gentiles who did not work at the collective farm had no access to food. They were dying at an alarming rate. Stalin wanted to force the Ukraine into collectivism and did not allow sustenance farmers to keep their own food. As a result, the authorities took everything edible from common people, condemning the masses to hungry deaths. The countryside suffered a much worse fate then the urban areas because city pawnshops traded flour, rice, sugar, and other foods for valuables. People from Kalyus packed their own gold, silver, and anything else of value that they could find and made the long journey to the nearest city. Some villagers had gold teeth or crowns removed and traded them to feed their families. I remember my grandmother making several such trips to Mogilev Podolsk and bringing back precious food to keep us alive.

My parents worked at the Jewish communal farm at this time. Since Stalin's aim was to force collectivism, his cronies confiscated all food from independent subsistence farmers. Collective farms also gave their food to the authorities but were allowed to retain enough to keep their workers alive and able to do farm work. My parents' pay was a bowl of soup and a piece of *mamaliga*[2] for lunch as well as some buckwheat flour to take home. I was a small child and did not directly receive any food from the farm. My parents took me to the lunchroom with them and sat me in between. I ate a spoonful from my mother's plate and a spoonful from my father's. But my mother could not stand to see her family hungry and sneaked in extra spoonfuls from her plate. She felt sorry for my father who worked very hard and bore hunger with great difficulty. His farm brigade grew tobacco, and he had to carry water from the Dniester to irrigate the crops. I remember his telling me: "I cannot survive this famine and will die right in the field."

Despite this, my father did everything possible to feed his family. One spring day the forecasters from the regional center predicted frost during the night. The delicate grape crop could not survive the cold, and the foreman asked for volunteers to keep fires burning around the grapevines at night. The pay for the work was an extra kilogram of buckwheat flour. Uncle Yankel and my father volunteered. Once the fires were burning, my father and my uncle lay down on the ground during a very still, moonlit night. They could hear the distinct sounds of a Jewish wedding on the Romanian side of the Dniester. They heard music, songs, joyous laughter, and even singular voices of the happy people. They were grown men but could not help weeping like children because happiness

---

[2] *Mamaliga* is a Romanian dish made from yellow corn. It is better known to the rest of the world in its Italian form, polenta. *Mamaliga* is one of the main traditional dishes of Romania. Historically a peasant food, it was often used as a substitute for bread or even as a staple food in the poor rural areas. Jews in the region adopted the food into their own cooking.

was possible so close to hunger and poverty. There was a place just across the river where people could rejoice and not worry about surviving until the next day.

I do not know how we survived until fall, but I clearly remember that after the harvest my parents received a lot of grain from the farm. My father took it to the mill and brought back flour. My mother baked so much bread that we could finally eat as much as we wanted.

I remember other handiwork of Stalin's henchmen. One day not long after the famine, I awoke to find out that my father was not home. I asked my mother where he was. She replied that he would return soon. However, I could detect a sense of worry in her voice and wondered whether my father was okay. He came back a few days later looking very tired, dirty, and unshaven. He picked me up, hugged me, and started crying, telling me that he never expected to see his family again. He had been held for ransom. This was a time of rapid industrialization in the Soviet Union, and the government needed gold and foreign currency. If the regional authorities suspected someone of having valuables, they put them in jail and interrogated them until they gave up whatever they had. I do not know whether my family had any money. If we did not have it, we must have found a way to get it—because my father would not have been released otherwise.

The Ukrainian nationalists created a police unit formed from the local Ukrainian population. This unit and others in neighboring villages would later be part of the guard of the concentration camps and ghettos and would actively and willingly take part in the murder of their Jewish neighbors. These Ukrainian separatists called a meeting of the Ukrainian population of the village as soon as they arrived. They declared that Soviet rule of the Ukraine had forever ended, and that the Ukrainian population would willingly submit to German rule. They said that the Ukrainian people should happily help the Germans deal with the Communists and Jews, who were the enemies of the Ukrainian and the German people. They blamed the Jews for all the hardships in the Ukraine and warned the Ukrainians not to go to Jewish homes because the Jews might poison or kill them. They bade the Ukrainians not to sell Jews food and so let the Yids (Kikes) starve to death. We were frightened and confused by these developments and did not know whether we would be better of with these Ukrainians or with the Germans.

I had spent the last year studying in the Ukrainian school because in 1940 the Communist authorities closed the Jewish school. It was part of their assault on religion and religious education. I found the transition to the Ukrainian school very difficult at first. At the Jewish school, all subjects had been taught in Yiddish. While I understood Ukrainian, I could not speak it well. However, I quickly conquered the language barrier and again became one of the best students in the class—especially in mathematics.

But now our Ukrainian neighbors and classmates, with whom we had grown up, started treating us with distrust, and some started to hate us. However, the police force was made up of decent people who treated us tolerably well most of the time. But trouble came from a different and completely unexpected place.

Romanian soldiers from Bessarabia crossed the Dniester River and started robbing the Jewish village. Two locals, who helped them translate and carry away their loot, assisted them. They plundered for two weeks and took everything they could find. The two local thugs knew everyone and told the Romanians exactly whom to rob and what to take. Neither the new authorities nor the police units wanted to enter into conflict with armed Romanian soldiers and stood aside during the looting.

It was about this time that we had our first causalities. Vendl Fryman, the father of a classmate, and his father-in-law decided to visit their relatives who lived in Staraya Ushitsa. They did so despite the new Nazi occupation laws that forbade the Jews from travel outside their villages. They made it to their destination but were caught and shot on the way back. It took a lot of money to convince the Ukrainian police to return their bodies to their family. All the Jews in the village came to the funerals.

The men who were mobilized during the first days of the war started returning. They were mostly Ukrainians who had been surrounded and taken prisoner. During the initial battles, the Germans captured whole armies. The German advance into the Soviet Union was so quick that many soldiers were captured before reporting to their posts. The only thing slowing the Germans down was the vast number of prisoners. In fact, because they could not hold so many prisoners, they were letting the captured men go home if they lived in territories that had already been captured by the Germans. The exceptions to this rule were high-ranking officers, party officials, and Jews; the Germans shot these on the spot. Many commanders simply changed into ordinary soldier's clothing to escape immediate death. Likewise Jews whose appearance did not betray them changed their last names to non-Jewish ones. If their comrades did not expose them, they managed to escape execution.

One morning before dawn somebody knocked at our window. My mother looked out and gasped at the sight of my father. He looked terrible. He had lost a lot of weight and was unshaven, dirty, and wearing an old shirt and torn pants. He was barefoot and his feet were bleeding. My mother boiled some water and he shaved, washed, and changed into clean clothing. He was very hungry, and my mother fed him the little we had left.

After my father regained a little strength, and we got over our initial shock, he told us what had happened. His unit was surrounded and lost communication with its regional command. The field commanders told the soldiers to walk off the battlefield into the forest one by one. My father and a Ukrainian from Gorachensy, the village nearest to Kalyus, wandered through the forest for two weeks. They avoided the roads because they were full of German military units. The Germans had already advanced so far into the Ukraine that it was impossible to join the fight at the current front because it was well beyond walking distance. My father and his companion could not travel safely in their uniforms and stopped in some village where an old man gave them some old clothing. They decided to head home. After coming back, my father spent two weeks in bed trying to recover. After some time, Uncle Yankel also came home under similar circumstances. His unit had been taken prisoner, and he barely got home alive.

Kalyus' remoteness allowed Hitler's New World Order to come to us a little later. However, by the time my father returned, the Germans had wrought their malice on us. A police unit of roughly fifteen young men from other villages was sent to Kalyus. The unit's leader was a very cruel man from the western part of the Ukraine. The policemen had come back from German captivity and willingly chose to serve the occupiers. Their arrival marked the true beginning of our suffering. They started forcing intense labor on us. They had us chop down trees, fix railroad tracks, and do other humiliating and utterly pointless work. This included moving snow from one side of the road to the other, just to put it back the next day. The women cleaned the policemen's homes and washed their laundry. The chief purpose of this labor was to torture us. The Jews were neither allowed to leave the village nor to visit one another after dark. No medical care was provided for us, and the physician's assistant, the only person qualified to give medical aid in Kalyus, was not allowed to visit Jewish homes. When the policemen set up their living quarters, they took furniture from Jewish homes. From our home, they took two beds, which my parents had bought right before the war started.

One Saturday morning, two Nazi-appointed Ukrainian government officials came to us from the regional center. They took ten hostages, including my father, with the help of the local police. Their demand was 25,000 rubbles (a sum more than three times what my father earned per year before the war) by the end of the next day. They threatened, in case we did not pay this ransom, to shoot the hostages. The people of the village were always very poor, and even more so now when nobody was allowed to work. Finding this sum would be almost impossible. However, everyone knew the hostage takers were not bluffing, and that all the hostages would indeed be shot if they did not receive the money. The most respected people in the village and the families of the hostages went from home to home and collected people's last pennies. At the end of the next day the village gave everything it had to the officials. The officials returned the hostages, whom they had held without food or water in a cellar for forty-eight hours.

After this, other government officials came to demand gold and money and everyone complied, giving up everything they had left despite living at the brink of starvation. We were only trying to survive until the next day and bought ourselves out of trouble when we could. The local policemen were not to be outdone by their leaders and always demanded we give them something or other. Day-to-day life became unbearable. We were not paid for our forced labor and did not have money to buy food. People gave away their last possessions for a little food, as meager as a few kilograms of flour and a few potatoes.

The policemen continued to torment us by always thinking up newer forms of humiliation. They ordered us to wear yellow circle marks on our overcoats as well as on our shirt shoulders to make us immediately recognizable as Jews. Those who resisted this marking were punished. A Jew who met a policeman was required to take off his hat and bow until his back was parallel to the ground. They beat us at every step without any sort of provocation. As bad as the situation seemed, it was about to get worse.

Full German authority was established at the end of October 1941. Only then did we wholly comprehend the meaning of the Nazi New World Order. The Germans did not rob us; there was nothing left to take. They did, however, double our abuse and humiliation. Now we had both the Germans and the policemen, and the Ukrainian policemen became even crueler to please their German masters. At this time we no longer had a synagogue, and the old Jews gathered in one another's homes for prayer. The Germans found out about this practice and raided the home where a prayer service was being held. They ordered the old Jews out of the house and commanded them to set the Torah scroll on fire. The devout Jews refused to desecrate our sacred book. They paid dearly for their disobedience; they were shot to death. The Germans set fire to the prayer books themselves. As warning to the rest, the Germans did not allow burial of the dead for two days, fully aware of the Jewish custom to bury our dead right away.

We lived in constant fear and did not know what the next day might bring. When winter started, it brought new hardships. Before the occupation we heated our homes by burning wood and straw. But now we could get neither because we could not leave Kalyus, nobody was permitted to trade with us, and we had not money to buy it, and we were cold and starving. People started dying of starvation, pneumonia, and exposure to the cold. The very young and old were the first to die. My brother Isaak became very ill. I do not remember the exact illness but only that he had a very high fever, and my parents were terribly scared. Victor Kulchitsky, our physician's assistant and the only person with medical training for many kilometers, was not allowed to visit Jewish homes or provide any type of care. My father went to beg him to see the child. Victor had lived in Kalyus for many years. He knew all the Jews by name, had visited every house, and cared for all the children as they grew up. Before the war, I attended school with his son Jeora and, on multiple occasions, had been a guest at the Kulchitsky house. Victor was a good person and despite his fears for the safety of his own family he could not turn sick people away when they needed his help. He came to our house at night and examined Isaak. He shook his head and told my parents that the child needed to go to the hospital. He prepared several medicinal powders and told us he would return to see my brother soon. Victor came a few more times, always late at night, and Isaak got better under his care until the danger completely passed. Victor visited other families too at night. These were heroic acts, because he helped us at great risk and could expect to receive nothing for his kindness other than our gratitude.

Winter brought hardship and death, but when spring came the situation did not improve. Our tormentors once again forced us to work and took every opportunity to humiliate us. The Germans were not the only ones inflicting punishment on us; as I said earlier, our former neighbors, the policemen, were even worse.

At the beginning of April, the police rounded up about thirty teenagers, including me, and told us to take enough food for several days of work outside the village. My mother packed some cooked potatoes, a half loaf of bread, and a water bottle in a sack. This was all the food my family could spare for my journey. This was about the quantity of food each one of us took. We reported to the square, and the guards made us walk to the village of Struga, which was twenty kilometers away. We spent the night sleeping in a horse stable and went to work on a nearby railroad in the morning. We spent the next two weeks following the same routine, closely watched by the policemen. Our food ended long before our work did. We would have died of hunger if not for the kindness of the local Ukrainians. They pitied us and brought us food. After we finished the work, we walked back to Kalyus. We returned to our families, who had lost the hope of ever seeing us alive again, hungry and half-dead.

A little time passed, and the policemen gathered us again for distant work. My mother and the rest of the family were very worried about my father's health and made sure the policemen did not see him. Fortunately, he was able to evade them. This time, the policemen told us to bring a kettle, an aluminum bowl, a spoon, and a few changes of clothing in addition to our food. None of us knew where the policemen were taking us or when we would return. Before leaving, I ran to say goodbye to my grandparents. My mother, sister, and brother walked to the square, the designated meeting place for about eighty young men and women. I said goodbye to my family. I did not think I would see them again. It was May 30th, 1942. I will never forget that day.

We marched to Novaya Ushitsa under the guard of a police envoy. In the evening we arrived at a Jewish ghetto in the city. Two rows of barbed wire enclosed several streets where the entire Jewish population of the town was forced to live. Policemen guarded the ghetto around the clock. Jewish policemen, who were assigned by the Ukrainian authorities, kept order inside the ghetto. These Jewish policemen assigned their people to labor and conveyed the orders of the German command to the populace of the ghetto. The ordinary inhabitants of the ghetto told us that the Jews running the ghetto were very cruel to them.

The men guarding us forced us into a large stone shed where we spent the night. The next day a group of young men and women from Zamighov, a neighboring village, were thrown into the shed. Like us, they had no idea where they were being taken next. At the end of our second day in the ghetto, we were taken to a square where local men and women were already awaiting departure. Five trucks drove into the ghetto with twenty policemen, four per truck; they divided us and loaded us onto the trucks. The drivers of the trucks were German. As night fell, we were driven off into the unknown.

We stood so closely huddled together that we could not turn. The night was quiet and warm, and we passed by quiet, sleeping villages. We were not permitted to speak. Each of us was thinking the same thing—where are we being taken? What new torment have the Germans thought up for us?

At some time after midnight the trucks stopped in a field. The guards ordered us to get out. They took us to the bushes in groups and allowed us to relieve ourselves. They then told us to get on the ground. We slept there until the sun came up. At dawn the policemen pushed us back into the trucks, and we rode on.

In the morning, the trucks pulled into, and stopped in, some town with a gate and fence made of barbed wire. The guards from inside the gates opened them, ordered us inside, and led us to a large square. We formed into two rows of men and women and waited for the commandant of the camp. The large young German soon appeared carrying a rubber baton. He spoke through an interpreter and announced that we had arrived at a work camp. He told us the rules of the camp. We will receive a number that will replace our name, and we are to carry this number at all times. We must provide this number at once if asked by the commandant, camp guards, and police, or work supervisor. Each day we will rise at six in the morning and report to the square for inspection. From there the guards will take us to work. We must work diligently. Upon completion of the day's work we will receive a bowl of soup and two hundred and fifty grams of bread at the camp kitchen. Curfew was at ten in the evening, and we must be in our barracks by that time. The men are not allowed to visit the women's quarters and vice versa. The punishment for violation of any camp rules was twenty-five blows from the commandant's baton or solitary confinement. Skipping work, not working hard, or breaking any work rules was the strictest offense and would result in being shot to death. Attempted escape resulted in immediate execution by hanging in the middle of the camp, as well as the execution of every tenth person in the escapee's work brigade. Finally he explained that we would be released at the completion of the work, and that the length of our stay was entirely dependent on us. After these and many more threatening declarations, he turned us over to the camp police, young Jews armed with sticks.

They handed out small pieces of cardboard with our identification numbers. They then led us to our sleeping quarters. These were old wooden barracks with no electricity, light, or heat. When we came to our designated space, each of us had to pick a spot on the straw covered floor. The people from Kalyus clung to one another in this frightening new place, and we took comfort in sleeping next to one another. This became our sleeping and living space. We sat on the floor, feeling defeated, tired, and hungry. We ate the food in our bags and talked about our present situation. It is true that we were scared, but we were also curious. We did not know what sort of place this was or what type of work awaited us. We did not even know the name of the town. Finally we decided to walk around the territory of the camp and find out what we could.

This is what we learned during our walk. The camp stood at the site of a former monastery. It was surrounded by tall stone walls on three sides; the forth side consisted of a barbed-wire fence and locked gate. The whole camp was in turn surrounded by two additional rows of barbed wire. The wooden barracks where the camp prisoners lived were built around a stone church. There was a large square in the middle of the camp. A well stood at the side of the square that was closest to the barracks. Big buckets of water flanked the well. Two guards wearing military uniforms were stationed outside the gates. Two towers manned by armed guards overlooked the entire territory of the camp. We feared drawing unnecessary attention and decided to return to our sleeping quarters. I lay down and started thinking about what had happened in the last few months, weeks, and days. The chaos and cruelty of it all caught up to me, and I started to cry. I was very afraid. I was still only a boy.

The end of the day came, and workers streamed back into the camp. They were organized into work brigades and marched into the square in neat rows. We joined them in the square and waited. The commandant appeared and walked the rows. He occasionally pointed at a worker with his baton. The policemen dragged the chosen person aside and the commandant beat him with his rubber stick. I never learned what offense, if any, the men had committed. After this was over, the policemen led the brigades to the kitchen for their daily portion of soup and bread. Through a small window, the kitchen staff shoved these meager meals at the prisoners. The workers returned to their barracks and ate their dinner. We did not receive food that first day, as we had not worked.

The returning prisoners questioned us about life outside the camp. They all had families somewhere and were desperate to find out what was happening. We in turn asked them about life in the camp. I found out that the camp was located in the Ukrainian town of Letichev.

The prisoner population at the Letichev camp numbered about two thousand five hundred Jews from the Kamenets-Podolskaya and Vinitskaya oblasts. Most had been at the camp for a month or less. The work was laying railroad tracks between the towns of Proscurevo and Vinnitsa, a key German supply route, as well as mining and breaking stone in the quarry. The work was difficult, and the guards were abusive. These guards were Lithuanians who had earned a reputation among the camp population for their cruelty. They beat the workers for any reason and often without any reason at all. There was also another group of prisoners who worked inside the camp. They worked in the kitchen, poured water into barrels used for drinking and washing, cleaned the camp, and handled all the work needed to keep the camp running. The work was much easier but getting into this work brigade was impossible, because it consisted entirely of relatives and close friends of the Jews in leadership roles at the camp.

My new comrades advised me to go to sleep as early as possible because the daily wake-up call consisted of screams and blows by the camp police. I would then need to get dressed quickly, run to the well, and then take my place in the work-brigade lineup in the square.

The next morning was just as the experienced prisoners had promised. At six in the morning, I awoke to screams and stick blows from the camp police. After dressing quickly, I grabbed the rest of the food left from home and ran to the water buckets. There was only time for a quick rinse at the well because of the large crowd gathered there. We then assembled at the edge of the square where the camp police assigned us, the new arrivals, to existing work brigades. I had to remember my place and row, and any lapse in memory was met with blows. Sticks were used to bring the assembly to order. The commandant appeared, rubber baton in hand. He walked around and looked over the brigades, beating anyone he did not like that morning. After this, he gave us over to the Lithuanian guards who loaded us onto trucks and drove us to a worksite outside the camp.

The police assigned me to the brigade that worked in the stone quarry. The quarry was located in the forest not far from the main road. Local Ukrainian volunteers dynamited the rock. We then picked up the large pieces, broke them into smaller pieces with sledgehammers, and loaded them onto wagons. Next, we pushed the wagons on rails to the road where we unloaded them onto waiting trucks. The wagons and trucks formed a nonstop conveyor. The guards were obsessed with keeping the conveyor running smoothly, and anyone who disrupted the rhythm would be in for a very rough time. The guards announced a break at noon. Workers sat on the ground and ate any food they had from the night before. Four prisoners pushed a wheelbarrow carrying a large bucket of water. We were able to drink for the first time since morning. The break offered a 30-minute rest from the nonstop conveyor. Almost nobody managed to make it through a day without being hit by a fist or a stick. I was quickly convinced that everything I had heard about their cruelty was true.

At the end of the day, about seven in the evening, we were loaded into the trucks and driven back to the camp. The camp police took charge of us at the gates. Once again we gathered at the square and received our blows from the commandant. Next it was time for my first meal from the camp kitchen. The bread was mostly made of parts of grain that were not supposed to be made into bread. There was very little actual flour in it. The soup was mostly water with a few pieces of potato, beets, and buckwheat floating in it. I was so exhausted that I was barely able to get to my spot in the barracks. I ate my soup and licked the plate. I was so hungry, but could only allow myself to eat half my bread. If I did not save some of the bread for breakfast, I would not have the strength to work. I was not always able to maintain my discipline. It was difficult for me to fall asleep hungry while I could feel the piece of bread, wrapped in a rag, under my head. Sometimes I ate the other half, piece by piece, during the night.

I worked in the quarry for three weeks. During that time, the women were taken out of the camp and moved to an unknown location. They were replaced by a group of new men. I would not have been able to withstand the difficult quarry work for very long. I knew I would soon fall down from exhaustion and, if I were lucky, the guards would shoot me instantly. If I were not, they would slowly beat me to death as they had often done with those who no longer had enough strength left to work. However, a miracle happened. The camp police transferred me to the brigade responsible for laying railroad tracks. The work there was not easy—and there were the same abusive guards—but compared to the work in the quarry, it was a lot easier.

Many Ukrainians from surrounding villages worked on the railroad. They were trained at laying railroad tracks and were volunteer workers. We assisted them by leveling the ground, carrying rock, and doing other unskilled labor. The Ukrainians were generally young men who had returned from POW camps. The Germans and Lithuanians treated them well and never abused them. Some of these workers were very sympathetic to us when they saw the guards abuse and beat us. Of course, they did not dare stand up for us, but even though they were not allowed to give us food and we were not allowed to accept it, many of them tried to leave something of their lunch for us to eat. Sneaking us food was risky for them because they would have been in trouble if the guards ever saw them doing this.

I quickly got used to getting hit with fists, sticks, and butt ends of rifles. We were hit all the time and stopped paying attention to it. The beating was far worse when the guards took the worker's number. When the commandant received the number back in the camp, he decided on a punishment. Often the punishment was twenty-five lashes. The Jewish camp guards carried out the beatings in the main square, for all to see. Some prisoners feared this punishment and refused to give their numbers to the guards. A young man from Kalyus, by the last name of Malamoud, did not respond when a guard screamed for his number. The guard shot him dead on the spot.

When a prisoner was killed outside the camp, we brought him back to be counted along with the living. The count had to be the same at the end of the day as it was in the beginning. The dead were thrown into a ditch by the camp wall and covered with a thin layer of dirt.

Sunday was our only day off from work. We spent most of the day washing and mending our clothes. We did not have soap to use on our bodies or clothing and washed only with water. By now it was summer, and it took our clothes a full day to dry. Whatever time we had left, we spent trying to rest in the barracks to gather enough strength for another week of work. It was also a good idea to stay out of the sight of the camp guards. Spotlight projectors mounted at the top of the two watchtowers lit up the camp. However, the barracks had no light, and we went to sleep and awoke in complete darkness.

One morning, two young Ukrainians, who worked two hundred meters ahead of the rest of the workers, preparing the ground for railroad tracks, came to look at my brigade. They needed four workers to assist them. The Ukrainians could pick the workers on the condition that they would take them to the brigade at the beginning of the day and return them at the end of it, bearing full responsibly for the prisoners during the day. I do not know what criteria they used to pick the helpers, but I was among the four. What I do know is that they saved me from certain death. My body could not have borne the intense physical labor for long. I remember these Ukrainian boys standing before my eyes, and I still remember their names; they were each named Grisha. One of them was a twenty-two-year-old, lefty, of average height, with a round face full of freckles. The other was a tall twenty-year-old with black hair and kind eyes. When I was with them, the work was calm; nobody guarded, beat, or rushed us. The Grishas turned out to be good people and treated us well. They brought their lunch from home and fed us as well. Usually it was cooked potatoes and, sometimes, even bread with real butter. We worked with them during the summer, and they often shared fruit with us. I was no longer hungry and could confidently eat my evening portion of bread and soup without worrying about going hungry the next day. My spirits lifted, and I hoped to live to finish the work and return home. I missed my family. I dreamed about them every night. I had never spent so much time away from them.

At the end of one day in August, after the usual activities at the square, I noticed new people at the soup line. Among them were a few people from Kalyus. I ran to them to find out if any of my relatives were among them. They told me that Uncle Yankel and my grandfather's brother and his two sons, Friedel and Razer, were in the camp. Uncle Yankel was my father's brother. I pushed through the crowd until I found him. When he saw me, he hugged me frantically and started crying. I could feel that something terrible had happened. I took him aside and said: "What's wrong? Why are you alone? Where is my father?" He started crying even more and said: "We have nobody anymore. Moyshele, you and I are the only ones left. Everyone else was shot." Everything went dark, and I felt as if a truck hit me. I was hysterical for a long time. I could not calm down. After a time, my uncle was able to get me off the ground. I took his hand and walked unsteadily to the barracks. I made a place for him on the floor next to me. We sat down, and I asked him to tell me what had happened.

He told me about everything that had happened since the day I left home. This is what I remember of what he said:

Right after I left Kalyus, it became a ghetto. The Germans enclosed a few streets with barbed wire, and all the villagers were forced to live there. My parents' house was outside the fence, and my family and other relatives went to live in my grandparents' house, which was within the appointed territory. A Ukrainian woman, a neighbor of ours, came to live in our house. She promised to keep everything as it was and return the house to us as soon as the war was over. The ghetto made life in Kalyus even more difficult than before. It was very crowded; five or six families lived in each house. They were guarded, and nobody was allowed to leave except a few people whom the guards put to work outside the ghetto every day. There was nothing to eat. The workers traded whatever things they had left, with the Ukrainians, for some food and secretly brought it back inside. These few crumbs fed the entire population of the ghetto. At that time, my grandfather became ill and paralyzed. He could not move at all.

Life in the ghetto was desperate not only because of the food shortage and overcrowding, but also because of the humiliation. It was summer, and outside the ghetto everything seemed normal. The Ukrainians living in Kalyus walked the streets freely, laughed, and went to school. They had a good time and did not fear anyone. These were our former neighbors, classmates, and people with whom we had worked at the factory and the farm. They were free because they were Ukrainians, and we were behind barbed wire because we were Jews. They looked at us as if we were zoo animals locked in cages, not recognizing us as their former neighbors. Some threw rocks and laughed at us as they passed the ghetto. Where did these people find such hatred for us? We had lived in peace and friendship and helped one another for many years. The feeling of helplessness and unfairness hurt even more than hunger and poverty. Of course there were also those Ukrainians who threw food over the fence, but unfortunately, there were few of them. This was doubly so because the Germans would have dealt harshly with anyone helping Jews.

During the early morning of August 20th, 1942, the number of guards around the ghetto increased. Many of the policemen came from other villages. There were so many that they stood one step apart surrounding the whole ghetto. People inside knew something very bad was about to happen and hid in cellars and any other place they could find. At noon, the police came inside and started forcing everyone into the square. They searched everywhere and beat people. At the square they declared that the Kalyus ghetto was closed and said that everyone was to be transferred to Novaya Ushitsa. They had even arranged for transport for the ill. My uncle and father carried my paralyzed grandfather and placed him on a horse cart. The Germans from the local garrison arranged all the villagers in a column, surrounded them, and led them in the direction of Novaya Ushitsa. When the column started marching, everyone believed they were really being transferred. However, when the column turned in the direction of the river, everyone realized they were walking to their death. Cries and screams broke out, and the Germans and policemen attempted to bring order with sticks and the butt ends of their rifles. However, they could not stop the commotion. Finally, the guards brought the column to a ravine with a ditch at the bottom of it. They forced the people onto the ground in front of a deep ravine and surrounded them on the other three sides. Four Germans, dressed in SS uniforms held machine guns aimed at the crowd. The guards started picking people that were able to work. They picked my uncle, my great uncle, and his two sons. My father was also picked but he refused to leave his family.

The sun was setting, and some of the policemen took the people selected for work back to the ghetto. Just as they were out of sight of the crowd, they heard machine-gun rounds. On that day, the 20th of August of 1942, eight hundred and fifty Jews from the village of Kalyus were shot to death[3]. Among them were my grandmother, grandfather, mother, father, sister, and brother as well as many other relatives. As of that day, the Jewish village of Kalyus no longer existed.

_____

[3] This account is corroborated by the Soveit Extraordinary State Commission's findings. The commission was established to document the atrocities and events in every Soviet locality occupied by the Nazis. Under the direction of special NKVD (predecessor of the KGB) units, teams were to record the names of those killed. In most places NKVD personnel were assisted by local residents. These reports, handwritten in Russian, are organized geographically by republic, oblast (state), raion (county) and town. They were stored in the Central State Archive of the October Revolution in Moscow, with relevant copies in republic area archives. Until recently the records were not available for public viewing. These reports were microfilmed in Moscow by Yad Vashem in 1990. The United States Holocaust Memorial Museum (USHMM) in Washington has copies of these microfilms: 27 reels, [RG-22.002M]. In 1995, the Museum created a town index to the 1,450 localities covered by the reports. I consulted these reports for background and the historical record of my grandfather's story. A one-page typed letter documented the excavation of the mass grave in Kalyus. The commission put the number of dead at 450 rather than the 850 cited by my grandfather. It turned out that many of the villagers had either died earlier or where taken to other ghettos and shot there. The report also indicated that the Germans did not shoot the children, as grandfather had assumed in his memoir, but threw them into the ditch and buried them alive.

The Jews of the Novaya Ushitsa ghetto were murdered the same day—August 20th, 1942.

The Jews of the Korelavets ghetto were murdered the next day—August 21st, 1942. The only Jews who remained alive were those who were considered by Germans able to work. They were all taken to Letichev.

When the guards brought my uncle and the others back to the ghetto, they locked them all together in one house. Somehow my uncle managed to run into my grandparents' house and take a few things with him. He brought these things to Letichev, and they helped him get by. My uncle did not know that I was alive and could never have fathomed that we would meet once again. Nobody at home knew where I had been taken.

We cried together the whole night. In the morning we awoke to the same wake-up call, blows, sticks, everything the same as before. My uncle and I ended up in different brigades. I reported as usual but could not work at all. I cried for my family all the time. I loved them so much and I could not live without them. I was still a child and needed my parents. Before that day, I had dreamed of finishing my work and going home to my loved ones. Now there was no home and there were no loved ones. I understood that we would never leave this place alive. Both Grishas tried to calm me down, but what could they say? What happened was terrible and irreversible. How could I live without my family? I cried and called for my parents at night. Uncle Yankel woke me and tried to comfort me. Even in my dreams, I could not accept the idea that my family was no longer alive.

I spent a lot of time thinking about my father's decision to share the fate of his family. At that moment, he likely did not think of me. He could not have known I was alive and needed him. He could not have known that we could have met. He stayed devoted to his family until the end. Not everyone could have acted as my father had. Some had left their wives and children at the edge of the grave. In the camp, there was a couple who had four young children. These children met death in the arms of other parents. Their parents were later shot in Letichev, but they cried for what they did until their last days, regretting that they did not stay with their children. Nobody can be judged; everyone has the right to die, not willing to survive his or her family, despite the full knowledge that this action will not be able to help the family at all.

At that time the summer was ending. It was nearing four months since I had arrived at the camp. Many of the people who came to the camp with me were dead. Some died of hunger and impossible labor, while others died at the hands of the guards. I was alive because I worked with the Ukrainians, who fed and pitied me, especially after they learned that I was an orphan. I also survived because my uncle stayed close to me and watched over me.

We could not wash ourselves properly during this entire time. There was no soap. We drank out of the same water barrels in which we washed our clothes and bodies. We never changed the straw lining on which we slept, and it was full of lice. An epidemic of typhus and dysentery broke out in the camp. The guards locked the poor people who fell ill with these diseases in the isolator—a freestanding building on the campgrounds. They were given neither food nor water, and passersby could hear their agonizing screams. When the isolator was full, trucks came to take the people away while we were at work. The brigade that worked inside the camp was forced to load these unfortunate souls onto the trucks. The trucks then took the ill to be shot in the forest. The transfer to the forest was not an attempt at concealment by the Germans but a matter of convenience; they brought back clothes of the victims for the prisoners to use. There was not enough room in the camp for a mass grave.

At that time the work on the railroad ended. I moved to a brigade responsible for digging ditches for underground cables going to the city of Vinnitsa. I was moved to this brigade so abruptly that I did not even get to say goodbye to the Grishas, my rescuers, the people who helped me survive until that time. However, I was destined to meet one of them later.

Now the hard labor started again. Once again, we were beaten and tortured by both the guards and the Ukrainian workers. Worst of all, I had to survive on the meager camp rations, one bowl of soup a day and a piece of bread. But at least my uncle was near. His brigade was still working on the railroad. Somehow he was occasionally able to trade things he brought from home with the Ukrainians for a bit of food. He secretly brought food back to the camp and shared it with me.

Every day the amount of work decreased as the railroad neared completion, and so the camp had excess workers. The Germans did not keep extra people in the camps, and they started to purge the camp of the weakest prisoners. Every day the commandant examined the work brigades and picked the feeblest of the workers. The police locked the condemned prisoners in the isolator with the ill and dying, and these were all taken to the forest and shot.

At that time, the camp's record keeping became very difficult because a large number of prisoners had died. My grandfather's brother and his sons decided to attempt an escape. They had lived in a Ukrainian village for many years before moving to Kalyus and looked and spoke Ukrainian. My great uncle was going deaf and pretended to be a deaf-mute. Once outside the camp, they would pretend to be Ukrainian workers returning from work in the coal-rich eastern Ukrainian region of Donbas. Their plan was to make a run while at work when the guards were not looking, get back to the Ukrainian village, and ask the locals to hide them. They decided to run during the first opportune moment. However, a morning purge got in their way. The father stood first in line, in front of his eldest son with the youngest behind. When the commandant started picking people to be purged, the elder son feared his father would be picked and quickly exchanged places with him. The commandant noticed this and called the son out of line right away. He was shot that day. The father was killed the next day, and the youngest son was shot when the camp was liquidated.

The time came for the Jewish New Year celebrations. I have no idea how the people in the camp could know that Rosh Hashanah and Yom Kippur had come.

I remembered my grandparents Iosif and Mira, who were deeply devout people and raised their children and grandchildren to love Judaism. My grandfather had started preparing me for my Jewish coming of age, the Bar-Mitzvah, a full year before I turned thirteen in 1940. At that time our synagogue had already been closed, and all religious ceremonies had been prohibited by the Soviets. My Bar-Mitzvah was celebrated very modestly and quietly at my grandfather's house in the presence of ten men (a minyan, or quorum for religious services). One of them had brought the Torah scroll, and my grandfather unrolled it on the table. I started reading the portion corresponding to that time of year. I had committed the passage to memory and read it in flawless Hebrew. My grandfather beamed with pride at the performance of his pupil. We then had wine and snacks, and everyone congratulated my grandparents, parents, and me. Everyone wished me to become a real Jew, a kind person who obeys the laws of the ancient Torah. I did not become a real Jew in the religious sense, because my environment did not allow it. This was also the last year I would have the guidance of my loving grandfather. But I have always tried to be kind to others and have, at least in my heart, always remained a Jew despite the many difficulties this choice entailed. Sadly I could not invite a single friend to my Bar-Mitzvah, because we were afraid we would be discovered by the Soviet regional authorities. My father would have lost his job, and I would have been expelled from school.

The prisoners clandestinely crowded into one of the barracks, much like Jews during the Spanish Inquisition, to ask the Almighty for his forgiveness and help. Muzen Flisher, the father of one of my classmates, sang the Kol Nidre prayer. He had a fantastic voice and sang the prayer with such grace and feeling that we all cried. His voice rose out of the darkness and begged the Almighty to rid us and our people of this endless torment.

On the day of Yom Kippur we assembled in the square as usual. I stood with my brigade for a long time before the guards told us to go back to our barracks. We were shocked: is it possible that the Germans are giving us a day of rest on Yom Kippur? However, we soon found out the reason, as we heard the cries of a large crowd. The Germans had decided to murder the Jews of the Letichev ghetto that day. Apparently the death march was to move through the area where we worked, and the Germans did not want the condemned to be able to escape death by blending in with us.

My young body started to break down under the heavy workload. Uncle Yankel was helping me a great deal by providing food and moral support; however, I could not expect to live much longer. I started to miss work. Sometimes I was able to hide from the camp police and return to the barracks. I lay there all day while the brigade was out for work. This was very dangerous. When the Germans came to collect the dying from the isolator they searched the barracks and took anyone they found there. They had no interest in keeping alive anyone who could not work.

It was during one of those days when I managed to skip work, that I heard the rumble of truck engines. I instantly knew I was in trouble because the Germans had come for their daily victims. I dashed to the kitchen where I ran into a woman from my village. I begged her to help me. She handed me two buckets and told me to bring her water from the well. If anyone asked her what I was doing, she would say that I worked in the kitchen with her. As I carried the water, I saw the Germans shoving the unfortunate people into the trucks. I also saw them go into the barracks and push out people who could not work and load them onto the trucks. However, nobody paid any attention to me. They believed me to be working and they left the camp.

After this, Uncle Yankel forced me to go to work every day. He would shove a piece of bread or cooked potato in my pocket. I held on for a little more, but soon I started feeling ill. My head became cloudy as if everything was shrouded in a fog. It was late autumn and it was getting cold outside. We were fortunate to have a steel worker in our barracks. He was able to construct a makeshift stove from the metal he tore off the roof. People brought splinters back from work, and we tried to keep warm.

Something positive also happened in the autumn. Ukrainian policemen replaced the Lithuanian guards. These new guards were no angels, but they were not as cruel as the Lithuanians. Some of them turned a blind eye when the prisoners brought food, that they were able to trade for with volunteer workers, back to the camp and did not confiscate it.

The sick and exhausted were no longer thrown into a separate building. They were allowed to die in the barracks lying in the lice-infested straw—their so-called beds.

At the end of one day, Uncle Yankel warned me that a major purge was to take place the next day. Uncle Yankel had a knack for getting this sort of information. His sources were a mystery to me, but I suspect he might have befriended some of the camp police. He bade me to go to work with his brigade. The next morning all the men that could stand got dressed, went to the square, and attached themselves to any brigade. Only three dying men, who could no longer move, remained in the barracks. The commandant examined the brigades one by one, pointing to the weakest men with his baton. He commanded the policemen to take them out of the rows and make them stand off to the side. After he finished purging each brigade it went off to work. It was my brigade's turn, and I could hardly stand. He instantly pointed at me, and the policemen dragged me out of line. When my brigade was leaving the camp, I was somehow able to sneak back into line. I was already at the gate when a policeman saw me and beat me out of line with his stick.

There were more than two hundred men chosen for death that day. We were locked in a barrack that was made up of several buildings. One of these buildings was the one where I had lived. There was only one exit from these buildings, and it was padlocked and guarded by police. Everyone knew that the trucks would come in several hours and take us to the forest where we would be shot. About fifty years have passed since that day, and I cannot remember all the things that I felt during that time, which I thought would be the last few hours of my life. I do remember that I was not afraid, and that nobody around me seemed scared either. Everyone was calm, and nobody screamed or cried. We were in a state in which nothing mattered anymore. We wanted it all to end as quickly as possible. There were eighteen people from Kalyus among the condemned. One of them was my relative Yaser. We had all lived in the same barracks and wanted to be together before dying. We came to our own building and sat on the floor. Everyone sat down at his own sleeping place and started eating the rest of the food. There was no reason to leave anything for tomorrow. But for some reason, Yaser and I did not feel like eating and left the building. We walked around the other buildings. We saw some people eat their reserves; others lay without moving and waited. Some others gathered in groups and spoke to one another. We spent a long time walking among these people and then decided to go back to our barracks. When we came back, we found the place empty save for a few dying men. The people from my village were all gone.

I do not know how the idea of a cellar came to me. I never knew cellars existed in these buildings. I certainly did not know one existed under our building. But when I saw that my countrymen were all gone, I turned to Yaser and said "They hid in the cellar. Let's find it and go there too!" It was as if an invisible hand sent us to the right corner because we found the hatch right away. We started banging on the floor and calling "Take us with you!" Suddenly the men lifted two boards and we went down. Everyone was there. Later I asked Uncle Yankel whether he had known about the existence of the cellar in the building. He answered that he did not know. Apparently some people had ripped out the boards ahead of time and prepared a hiding place just for such a scenario.

We lay in the cellar quietly, pressed up to one another, afraid to stir. After some time, we heard the sound of boots on the floor and the sound of the dying being taken away. We lay still for a long time. Finally we heard the steps and voices of the men returning from work. We climbed to the top. When my uncle, who had been out to work, saw me, he started crying. He had not expected to see me alive.

For unknown reasons, the condemned men were not taken to the forest that day, but locked in another building before the workers returned. Uncle Yankel and I agreed that I should hide in the cellar again the following day because the policemen might recognize me and put me in the isolator. I was not going to be able to find a way out of there. The next morning, Uncle Yankel put a piece of bread and boiled potato in my pocket and gave me a bottle of water. All the people who hid in the cellar the day before also chose to stay there again. When we went down to the cellar, someone stole the bread and potato out of my pocket. I did manage to hold on to my bottle. I was very ill at this time and had a hacking cough. When I coughed in the cellar, my accomplices almost suffocated me by pressing my face into the ground and covering my head with a jacket. I spent most of the day in this position. We only came upstairs once we heard the workers return again.

When we came upstairs, I saw that my uncle was not among the returning workers. The other prisoners told me the guards took him and nineteen others to cover the graves of the people who had been shot. I was suddenly jolted with the knowledge that the Germans usually shot the people covering the graves after they finished their work to eliminate witnesses of their crimes. But the Germans were not worried about witnesses now because they knew the camp would soon be liquidated. Uncle Yankel came back in a few hours.

Death was a regular occurrence to us. We saw it every day, every hour. Death awaited us at every step, and we had become desensitized to it. But what Uncle Yankel saw in the forest reached him and shook his very soul. He could not forget the victims lying in a ditch in pools of their own blood. He imagined his wife and children dying the same way back in Kalyus. He could not calm down for a long time. I was so exhausted and sick by this time that I existed in a sort of half-dream state. My own voice and actions seemed to take place outside my own wilting body. But Uncle Yankel's story shocked me out of that state. I was supposed to be in that ditch, had it not been for the miracle of that cellar. I suddenly awoke from my waking dream and wanted to live! I wanted to tear away from this hell and live!

I started thinking of a way to escape. While escape would be near impossible, the longer-term problem was finding a place to go. All the Jews who had lived for many kilometers around were either murdered or dying in Letichev. Most Ukrainians actively helped the Germans murder the Jews and could not be counted upon for help. Few Jews attempted escape because they could find no sanctuary. Given our state of starvation and physical ruin, it was hardly worth the effort. However, we heard a rumor that the Romanians left Jews to their own fate in their occupied territories. The Romanians still used Jews for hard labor and allowed them no rights but they did not kill them as a matter of policy. If I did manage to escape, I had no idea which way to run. I neither knew the area of Letichev, nor the direction to take to head for Romanian territory. I did know that Aunt Sonya, my mother's sister, lived in Kopaygorod in Vinitskaya oblast before the war. This was an area that I believed was in the Romanian territory. My maternal grandmother also lived near Kopaygorod before the war. I did not know whether she and her family were alive and, if so, whether they were still living in that same area. My uncle had met them before and knew who they were.

I offered my uncle the idea of staging an escape and finding my aunt or grandmother. The probability of success was low, but we had nothing to lose. Everyone knew that the camp would not be in operation for long and, by this time, nobody believed we would be allowed to leave. If we could only get to the Romanian land, we could save ourselves.

Uncle Yankel agreed with me, and we decided to try this plan. However, he did not know the area well, and I knew it even less. He shared the plan with the two people who lay near us—Shloyme Noodleman and Yasha, whose last name I do not remember. Shloyme was married to the sister of my uncle's wife, which made him and my uncle distant relatives. His wife and children were shot in Kalyus. Shloyme was a good choice for an accomplice because he knew the area well, he drove horses for the farm before the war, and he could pass for a Ukrainian. Yasha was deported from Bessarabia and lived in Kalyus with his mother and sister before coming to Letichev. His mother died in Kalyus, and his sister had been shot in Letichev.

We could not even consider taking Yaser. By this time he could barely stand and completely gave up on life. Fate was on our side because the time of year and situation in the camp made escape more plausible. Winter started early that year, and there was deep snow on the ground. There were fewer Germans on the roads, and the policemen stayed indoors close to their moonshine and warm kettles. The prisoners cleared snow from the railroad tracks. Our guards were less numerous than they had been and consisted of a few disinterested Ukrainian policemen. We were no longer counted when leaving and entering the camp. The Jewish camp policemen were no longer zealous as they had lost their illusions that their faithful service to the Germans would save their lives; they knew they would be shot with the rest of the prisoners.

We received our snow shovels in a shack about one hundred and fifty meters outside the camp. The interval of time and space spent getting our shovels would be most accommodating for escape. However, we agreed to make a run whenever the opportunity presented itself, not just at the shed. My uncle and I agreed that I should hide in the camp for the next few days to gain strength for the escape. We were gambling on nothing drastic happening during that time.

My uncle left me whatever food he could spare, and I spent that day lying next to the metal stove. A few more prisoners managed to sneak away from work and lay next to the stove with me. But we were not the only ones that liked warmth. When my uncle returned from work, he gasped when he saw that my black shirt had turned white with lice. He pulled the shirt off me and threw it in the fire. He forbade me to lie next to the stove.

My uncle, Shloyme, and Yasha spent nights whispering about our escape plans. I once awoke at night and heard Shloyme and Yasha trying to convince my uncle that I must be left behind. They argued that I was very weak, going blind, and would only be a hindrance to them. I was in fact quickly loosing my eyesight.

My vision first started to deteriorate when I contracted scarlet fever in fifth grade. Scarlet fever was a serious and communicable disease at that time, and I needed to go to an infectious disease hospital. Kalyus had neither hospital nor doctor; instead, Victor Kulchitsky cared for everyone in the village. The farm lent my father a cart and horses, and he took me to the hospital in Novaya Ushitsa. My fever was so high that I did not remember the ride to the hospital. I spent six weeks at the hospital recovering from this infection and, when I returned home, my parents noticed that my vision had significantly worsened. I went to Mogilev Podolsk to see the nearest optometrist. He examined me, prescribed eyeglasses, and told me to wear them when I study.

Lying on the cold floor, I felt anger swell inside me. Yasha and Shloyme had no hope for survival before presented with my escape plan. While we needed Shloyme, the only reason we asked Yasha to come with us was that he slept in our area, and we could not discuss escape without his knowledge. We asked him to come with us to keep him from giving us away. And now these two wanted to betray me and leave me to die? I was about to speak when my uncle hissed: "I left my wife and children to die. Do you think I will leave Moyshe here? He is the only reason I have left to live!" I was partially reassured, but part of me still feared that they might convince him to leave me. I pretended to be asleep and kept quiet.

In the morning, I confronted Yasha and Shloyme about what I had overheard. I told them that I was rested enough to go to work with them. But they insisted I stay in the camp, and not go to work, for several days. I knew well that the only chance at escape would come at work. Given what I had heard the night before, I was not going to lose my only chance by staying back. I shot back "If you do not take me to work with you, I will tell the police that you are planning to run! Take me with you. If there is a chance at escape, I will not lag behind. But if you find me a hindrance, you can leave me in the forest or some other secluded place. I do not care where I die!" I knew I could never really betray them by ratting on them, but I wanted to live and would not be left behind. From that time forward, I heard no more talk about leaving without me.

My uncle still had some of the valuables from home, and he took them to work in preparation for the escape. My vision had quickly deteriorated, and I was afraid to be away from my coconspirators. I kept very close to them at all times. We did not get the opportunity to run that day. The next day the guards drove us a long way from the camp to clean tracks. We worked in an open space and escape was impossible. We would have been spotted and shot right away. All our hopes lay in the return trip that night. By the time we approached the camp, it was dark. We returned our shovels at the shack and the column turned toward the camp. We slipped to the back of the column and waited for our chance. The column stopped at the gate and stood still. The two policemen watching the back walked to the front to see what was happening. They, like us, were very cold and wanted to return us, get to their warm homes, and get drunk. We did not hesitate, stepped out of line, and ran full speed to a half-destroyed house that stood nearby. We hit the ground and lay very still until all the workers and the policemen entered the camp. Everything became quiet, and I had a few moments to think. It was November 25, 1942. Six months earlier, the gates of this camp opened before me. I had spent the next one hundred and eighty days in hell. I was brutally abused by the German, Lithuanian, and Ukrainian guards and even by my own people, the Jewish camp police. I suffered from nonstop hunger and from intense labor. I was infested with lice, slept next to people sick with typhus, and did not catch it. Death crept behind me all the time and managed to grab me by the throat twice. The end seemed inevitable, but I somehow managed to save myself. I thought about all this and more while I lay in the cold. I had just turned fifteen a few days earlier, and I wanted so much to live. Stronger men than I had crumbled and lost their desire to live. But no matter what happened to my body, my will to live could not be completely broken. Perhaps I wanted to live more because I was younger than the rest and had yet to taste life. I do not know the reasons, but my will to live overcame all else and, at least for now, had kept three others alive in my wake.

But would I be strong enough to follow my journeymen, or would they be forced to leave me somewhere? Could we find the way to Romanian territory? Would my aunt and grandmother still be there? Are there any Jews left alive on Romanian territory, or was it all just a rumor? We had to travel through many villages all the while eluding both Germans and local police to find out.

After a time Shloyme Noodleman decided we should start moving. He was most familiar with the area and became our de facto leader. The only road we knew was to the village of Verbka, which was ten kilometers from the camp. We had worked there during the summer, and many of the Ukrainians from the village worked with us. We hoped to find somebody we knew to get directions to our destination. Getting around Letichev was very dangerous. The town was swarming with Germans and policemen. However, it was very dark, and we ran from house to house and started making our way out of town. We filed one by one in this order—Shloyme in front, then my uncle, then I, and finally Yasha in the back. We stuck to this order throughout our journey. We got out of Letichev without being detected and started walking along the train tracks toward Verbka. The temperature outside hovered around a devastating minus 25 degrees Celsius (minus 13° F), and railroad cars rarely passed over the train tracks. We walked very quickly in order to stay warm and arrived at the village around midnight. I had passed the first test by keeping pace with the others.

Every Ukrainian village home used to have a dog, but the Germans ordered all of them destroyed. This proved to our great advantage because the village was very quiet. It was extremely cold, and there was thick snow underfoot. The village was sleeping, but some windows were lit. We were trying to decide where to ask for directions, when we were suddenly surrounded by a group of young men. These were local boys who were on their way to have some fun. They asked us who we were, even though they guessed right away we were Jews from the camp, because there were no other Jews alive in the area. They decided to take us to the police. By this time I had no fear of death and had expected to die at any moment for many months. However, being caught escaping would surely mean a great deal of torture before death. This was my only fear now.

It was dark, and I could not see their faces but one voice sounded familiar. I remembered it well; it was the voice of the round-faced Grisha, the lefty with whom I worked all summer. I said "Grisha, don't you recognize me? It's me, Moshko (this is what the Grishas used to call me). This is my uncle. These two are my countrymen. Let us go!" He recognized me and asked about the other three men who had worked with us that summer. I told him two of them had been shot, and the other was still in the camp. He was kind and asked the others to let us go. He pleaded with them not to take such a sin on their souls. At first the rest of the young men refused to listen to Grisha but, after some pleading, they agreed. They made us promise that if we were caught, we would never mention them. They told us to leave the village immediately. Grisha had saved me again.

We left quickly, before they could change their minds. When we reached the edge of the village, we decided to knock on the door of a house where a light burned. We had no other choice—we needed to find out where to go. Shloyme knocked on the door while the rest of us hid in the courtyard. A middle-aged man came out, found out what was going on, and asked us to come into the house. We entered a very warm room with a burning stove. The man's wife, daughter, and son-in-law were also in the house. The master of the house asked us to sit and started to question us. We told him the truth—we escaped from the camp today and we were headed to the town of Bar. From there we hoped to get to Romanian-occupied territory. He told us that he hated Germans and was afraid his children would be sent to work to Germany. He also said he used to have many Jewish friends in Letichev. He then asked his wife to feed us, and she brought borscht and *mamaliga* from the stove. We started to eat greedily. Our hosts shed tears as they watched us. We were thin, dirty, and ragged. I was wearing torn remains of shoes which barely clung to my feet. My uncle's head was wrapped in a rag in lieu of a hat. We must have looked like animals devouring the food. We had not eaten warm food for a long time, and it was heavenly to us. This unexpected kindness made us relax, and we were suddenly very weary. We forgot about our difficult situation and did not want to leave this warm house or the company of these good people. The man understood all this and told us to sleep a little. We instantly fell asleep in a sitting position on a bench where we were resting. I do not know how long we slept, but it seemed too short. We were awakened by the man, and he told us it was time to go. The man gave me a pair of old shoes which were in much better shape then mine. He also gave my uncle and me hats with earflaps. The woman gave us a loaf of bread for the road. My uncle wanted to give them some of his valuables, but they refused. They did not need anything from us. We thanked them warmly for everything and said goodbye. They had taken a great risk: if the Germans or policemen found us in their house, their family would have been shot along with us. The man walked with us to show us the safest road to the next inhabited place, which was a gypsy village. He brought us to a safe path through the forest and told us not to fear the people in the next village. They also despised Germans and would show us the way forward. We thanked him again and plunged into the forest.

It was still intensely cold, but the forest was quiet, and the trees sheltered us from the frost. The moon had just come out, and it was bright as day. The ground, trees, and bushes around us were covered by untouched snow. The air was clean and smelled of pine. We had fallen into a fairytale kingdom, and our souls felt at peace. This was also true because we had found good people who fed and warmed us. It had been so long since we had seen real, human life. Four unfortunate, dirty, and ragged people watched this beauty as if charmed, and, for a moment, we forgot what we were running from and why we were there. This picture stands before my eyes even today. I feel I have seen such beauty only once in my life: the first night of freedom after the escape from the camp.

Shloyme's voice brought us back to reality, and we started to walk the road in the direction of the gypsy village. We were not afraid of meeting Germans because we knew they did not move around at night.

We also did not worry about locals because few traveled this road at night. The road we traveled was a little known path, and the night was far too cold for the Germans, who were unprepared for this climate. We walked quickly because we needed to get to the gypsy village before sunrise. We moved silently, not wanting to break the stillness around us. Each of us was alone with his thoughts. I do not remember what I thought about. It must have been about my family, whom I would never see again even if I managed to survive. I never stopped thinking about them.

We reached the village before sunrise. It was made up of only ten small, depressing-looking houses. The people were already awake, and an old man came to meet us. He invited us to his home without asking any questions. One room made up the entire house. A huge stove, the height of a person, burned inside, and it was very hot. An old gypsy woman sat beside the stove. There was no furniture in the room. The old man told us to sit down on the floor. We told him who we were and where we were headed. He asked us if anyone had seen us. Satisfied when we said no, he asked the old woman to put some potatoes in the stove. While the potatoes were cooking, we took off our wet shoes and jackets and spoke to the old man. He told us that there were no Germans nearby. They stationed themselves in towns and large villages. However, we had to stay mindful of police because they were in every village. He advised us to travel at the edge of villages and visit the houses on the fringes only if we desperately needed something. Under no circumstances were we to go into the village centers. He told us that the Germans were killing gypsies as well as Jews and had not yet gotten to his village. They had taken two of his sons, and he did not know where they were or even whether they were still alive. We asked him for directions, and he told us how to proceed and gave additional advice on how to avoid encounters. By that time, the old woman pulled the potatoes out and offered them to us by putting them at our feet. We ate them eagerly, burning our fingers and tongues. There were a lot of potatoes, and we could not eat them all. The woman told us to take them with us, and we filled our pockets and were able to keep our hands warm on them for some time. Dawn came, and we could remain there no longer. We affectionately thanked them and stepped back into the cold.

We walked in the forest for a long time. We climbed down into a ravine filled with snow and became trapped in it. We dug ourselves out with great difficulty and came back into the forest. Now it was past noon and too dangerous to keep walking. We walked a little further and found a fallen tree. After clearing some of the snow around the tree, we sat down against it and dumped out the snow in our shoes. We ate the potatoes but decided to save the bread which the woman from the previous village had given us for later. When we were walking we did not feel the bitter cold, but now it penetrated us right down to our bones. We were exhausted and started to fall asleep. We knew that if we fell asleep, we would likely freeze to death, but we had no strength left and let our eyes close. We would have certainly frozen to death if not for two women who stumbled upon us while looking for firewood. They understood who we were just by looking at us. They told us to leave quickly because there was a police headquarters near their village. Two weeks ago, the police caught a Jewish woman and her two children, a son and a daughter. They tortured them all night. In the morning they took them outside the village and shot them. The women showed us the path to the next village and bade us to stay hidden until night.

The path led us out of the forest into a meadow with several stacks of hay. We decided to hide in one of the stacks until nightfall. Shloyme said that if we made a hole in the hay, climbed in and filled the hole again we would be able to sleep all day and not freeze. We did this, and, when inside, huddled together for warmth. It was indeed warm inside, and we were able to nap until evening. After sundown, Shloyme decided to go into the village by himself to see if he could get some food and directions. He left, and we waited for him impatiently. Time dragged on painfully and, after quite a while, we felt he should have already come back. Suddenly we heard gunshots from the direction of the village. We feared that Shloyme had been discovered by the police and shot. We had given up hope of seeing him alive when to our amazement he returned unharmed. He climbed into the hole and told us that he was neither able to get food nor find directions. He knocked at the first door, and the person told him that the police in the village send all young men and women they come across to work in Germany. Shloyme quickly fled the village. On his way back, he also heard the gunshots but did not know where they came from.

We had no choice but to spend the night there. We still had the bread, split it equally among us, and ate. It had become hard as a rock because of the cold. We covered ourselves with hay and fell into a light sleep.

When we awoke, it was already morning. I climbed out of my hiding place and instantly felt the biting cold again. We started down the same path once again, unsure of where it led. While the Germans were not used to the cold and avoided unnecessary trips, the local police were unbothered and traveled freely from village to village. Our goal was to avoid such chance meetings, for obviously they would not turn out well for us. We walked for a long time before a small horse-pulled sled overtook us. Three women sat on the sled, and the horses were led by a coachman. They asked us where we were going. They offered to give us a ride to their village, which was on our way. We gladly accepted. We learned that they were coming from a baptism, and that their husbands had stayed behind with friends. The women had to return to feed their livestock. They knew that we were Jews because we could not conceal it. They showed great courage and kindness taking us with them. We rode for twenty kilometers and stopped at a fork in the road. One road led to their village and the other to our destination. Before parting, they gave us bread, cooked eggs, and apples. Despite the war and the presence of Germans, these people lived a normal life. They visited friends, slept in warmth, and did not fear anyone. And here we were, the most unfortunate people, chased from our homes, hunted and killed just because we were Jews. We envied them.

We had not eaten anything since morning and were famished because it was well after noon. However, we could not stop in this open place and needed to get to the forest. We walked quickly and ate on the move. We then spied a few houses near the road. We came to the edge of some village and could not go around it. There was no other road but the one that led right through. We hoped to get through unnoticed but were spotted by a man chopping wood in his yard. He called out to us and asked us who we were and where we were headed. We told him we were Jews and were headed to Bar. He started screaming that we were headed the wrong way, and that the whole village would suffer because of our presence. He continued screaming something about calling the police, but we were no longer there. We ran into the forest as fast as we could. We ran for a long time until we were out of breath. He most likely wanted to scare us, or he changed his mind about reporting us to the police. If he had gone to the police, they would have found us quickly. But my uncle felt that somebody was chasing us on horseback. He lay down on the snow and said that he would go no further. He decided that if he was going to fall into the hands of the police he preferred to freeze to death right there. Shloyme grabbed him by the collar and threatened to choke him to death on the spot if he did not get up. The threat worked, and Uncle Yankel came to his senses. He got up, and we walked on.

We followed a path that had been recently trampled in the snow and came to a large clearing. A fire burned in the middle of the meadow. Apparently somebody had worked here during the day and left the fire burning. We sat down around the fire, warmed ourselves, and ate the remainder of our food. The day was ending, and the forest grew dark. We saw a village as we left the forest but were afraid to go into it. We turned into another field and found more haystacks. We climbed into one using last night's experience and prepared to sleep. We whispered about the events of the day when we heard voices and the sound of approaching footsteps. We stopped talking and started listening. The voice was female. Shloyme moved some straw and glimpsed two women stuffing a sack at a neighboring stack. They were gathering feed for their animals. Shloyme decided to come out and ask them to take us to the village and feed us and, if possible, let us spend the night. He slowly climbed out and spoke to them calmly from a distance. He told them we meant them no harm and only meant to speak to them. He came to them, and they spoke to each other. We could not hear their conversation, but he soon motioned us to come over. We helped them stuff their bags and started walking toward the village. They walked in front, and we followed them. It was dark and as soon as we stepped into the village they dropped their bags and ran. We did not even see where they ran. Apparently they were afraid to turn us down but decided to flee as soon as the time was right. We had no choice but to return to our hiding spot. This was dangerous because the women knew our hideout and could easily lead the police there. However, we figured they would not do so because they would have to explain what they were doing in the field at night. They had obviously been stealing hay, and we figured that they were not eager to explain their actions. We climbed back into the only place we knew where we would not freeze to death. I was exhausted from the day's journey. The escape required intense, nonstop concentration. I lived from minute to minute and thought about nothing more than surviving the moment. While moving about, I did not allow myself to think about anything other than immediate survival. But as I lay to rest, I felt the heavy burden of the loss of my family, and the virtual impossibility of this escape plan that has such a minuscule chance at success. Surely death would come, and I hoped it would be quick and painless.

Snow fell that night and covered us. We barely climbed out of the hay the next morning. We found the road with difficulty because it was covered with fresh snow. Shloyme was a good guide and could instinctively find the right way. We came upon a small village and knocked at the first door we came to. A woman opened the door and let us inside. She poured borscht into a large bowl and gave us four wooden spoons. Likewise she took hot *mamaliga* from the stove and served it to us. The hot food and warm house were very comfortable, and we did not want to leave. However, the woman told us that she was afraid to keep us in her house for long. She told us we were now only twenty-five kilometers from Bar and could reach it before the end of the day. We thanked her for her kindness and went on our way.

The winter days were very short and ended before we could get far. Another kind person fed us in some village, and we were now only eight kilometers from Bar. We planned to reach it and cross into Romanian territory that night. As soon as we left the village, we caught up to a middle-aged man who was also walking in the direction of Bar.

We did not have to introduce ourselves as Jews, because our appearance gave us away. The man figured out who we were and asked us our destination. For some reason we trusted him and told him the truth—we were headed to Bar to cross the border into Romanian territory. He advised us not to go there. He lived in Bar and knew it to be swarming with Germans. All the Jews of Bar had been shot, and we could not pass through unnoticed. We would be spotted and killed quickly. He told us to take another road that went through a meadow. In five kilometers we would come to a single house surrounded by hay stacks. An old man lives there with his daughter. He told us to go to them and ask them to help us. They were good people and would not turn us away. However, he told us to be extremely cautious, because policemen from Bar rode their horses to buy hay from the old man. We believed the man and followed the road he suggested. It was all as he had described, and we came to the lone house in the hayfield. We knocked on the door, and the old man came out. We asked for his help, and he agreed to help us cross the border. But he told us that policemen from Bar were due to arrive to pick up hay. They always came at this time of day, and we would have to hide in his shed. He told us he would lock us in the shed, and after the police left he would introduce us to people who could help get us over the border.

We were at the old man's mercy and could not disagree. We went to the shack and dug ourselves into the hay and heard the padlock click behind us. We soon heard ringing bells and stomping hooves. We could hear the slurred voices of the policemen, and it was obvious that they were drunk. They walked into the house and returned with the old man.

We heard him tell them where to get the hay. For a moment, we appeared to be in a trap. The old man could turn us in and even receive a reward for catching four Yids. Fortunately he was a decent person and opened the door only after the drunks had departed.

He asked us to come inside the house. It was evening, and a kerosene lamp and a stove lit the room. His daughter worked at the stove. They asked us to sit at the table, and the daughter served us potatoes, sauerkraut, condensed milk, and bread. The old man bade us to be calm and not to hurry. Nobody else was going to come that day. He asked us if we were afraid that he would turn us in. We admitted that we did fear it. He laughed and said he would not have turned us in even if he were faced with death. The daughter told us that before the war she attended a school in Bar and lived in a Jewish home. She had many Jewish classmates and friends before the war. She was married but when the war started, her husband was drafted and she returned to her father's home. She and her father were able to save a few of her Jewish friends from Bar and get them to Romanian territory. They told us that the border, which was eight kilometers away, had been drawn by an arbitrary agreement and that there were no checkpoints or fences. It was patrolled by mounted German and Romanian soldiers on their respective sides. They also explained that patrols were infrequent at night, especially given the severe cold, and we would be able to get through.

The old man told us to go to a village located on the border. There were three fishermen there who would help us cross the border and give instructions on where to go from there. He then gave us bread and wished us well. We were very grateful to him and started toward the village. We had now walked for more than three days and were entering the last stage of our journey. Would we be able to make it?

The night was bright with moonlight, and everything was visible for kilometers. It was still bitterly cold outside. We could not let these things distract us, and we found the village quickly. Shloyme went to the house about which the old man had spoken. A window was open, and we could see the three men. One of them came out, talked to Shloyme, and agreed to help us. He recommended we go to another village nearby and locate a smuggler who took people across the border in exchange for money or valuables. We walked on and found the next village and the appropriate house quickly. A woman came to the door and told us that her husband was across the border on business. She said for us to come back the next evening. We answered that we could not wait, and she explained the best place to cross the border. We considered our options and decided we had no choice but to cross the border.

The crossing place was near a huge, brightly moonlit meadow. It was covered by untouched snow—with no trace of human or animal tracks. At the other side of the meadow we saw a railroad that was part of the German supply route. We would have to walk across the field, cross the tracks, walk a little more, and we would be on the Romanian side. However, to do so we would expose ourselves completely. The meadow was so large that we would be clearly visible for a long distance. Once again we had no choice but to continue.

We started walking through the field, immediately plunging into deep snow. We asked God for a few minutes of cloud cover, but the sky remained clear. We kept walking and walking until we reached the tracks.

We crawled over them because this was the most visible spot. We finally walked into the cover of the forest. We continued at a quick pace, trying to get as far from the field as possible. We stopped to catch our breath only when we got to the first village. By our calculations this village was on Romanian territory. We walked the empty streets not daring to knock at anyone's door. At last, we saw a small shed near one of the houses and decided to spend the night in it. The walls of the shed were old and punctured by many holes, and it was not really warmer in the shed than outside it. While it did not shield us from the cold, it did keep us concealed. I do not know how long we walked to get to this point, but we were drenched with sweat from the walk and the stress. My shoes were full of snow from walking in the field, and I had no opportunity to stop and clean them out. This snow had turned into ice and walking in these shoes had been the same as walking on ice barefoot. I found a clothespin and used it to scrape the ice out of my shoes. After some time we were really cold and starting to get frostbite. There were some corn leaves in the yard, and we used them to wrap ourselves. These leaves provided very little defense against the cold, but they were better than nothing.

At dawn a woman appeared out of the house. She had heard some sounds in the shed and yard at night but was afraid to come out in the dark. She got really scared when she saw us in her shed, but did not scream. We calmed her, and she asked us who we were and where we came from. We told her the truth, and she told us to leave the village right away. The village was, as we had expected, on the Romanian side. However, it was right on the border and Germans crossed over often.

We asked her for something to eat. She told us that she had two children and had nothing to feed them. She did not even invite us into the house to warm up.

We started walking to Kopaygorod, which was thirty-five kilometers away, with our teeth chattering from the cold. Although we had made it to Romanian territory, we did not feel safe yet. At noon we came to a village and knocked on the door of the first house. We asked the woman who answered whether she would feed us in exchange for some of my uncle's valuables. She offered us some *mamaliga* and milk. We sat on a bench and talked with the woman's husband while she cooked. We asked him whether there were any Jews living in the area. He said that some Jews who had been deported from Bessarabia lived a few kilometers away in former military barracks. These Jews traveled to surrounding villages to beg or trade for food. Those who were artisans offered their services in exchange for food. In fact, Jews sometimes came to their village. We were thrilled because it seemed Jews were, more or less, free to travel. The woman served us a large piece of *mamaliga* and poured us milk, and we sat down to eat and drink.

At that time, a man and woman knocked on the door and entered. We recognized them as Jews instantly. We jumped up in amazement. It had been a long time since we had seen Jews who could move around freely. They introduced themselves as tailors and asked our hosts whether they needed anything mended or sewn. We asked our hosts whether the tailors might join us at the table, and they consented. We fired endless questions at the tailors while we all ate. They told us that they were living in the former military barracks with more than four hundred other Jews from Bessarabia. When the Romanians reentered Bessarabia following the Soviet occupation, they deported all Jews.

The camp was not guarded by Romanians and had its own Jewish police and commandant to keep order. The residents of the camp survived on what they could hustle in the surrounding villages. We explained our situation, and the tailors invited us to spend the night at their camp. Kopaygorod was fifteen kilometers from camp, and we would be able to reach the city the next day. For the first time in six months, I felt safe and at ease as I realized that I had saved my life. Living Jews were present right in front of me. Yes, they lived at a camp, no doubt in terrible conditions, but nobody guarded them, and they were free to travel and find food. The tailor told us to be careful around Romanian gendarmes[4] who beat wandering Jews half to death when they ran into them. However, this did not scare us, as we had been constantly battered, and one more beating meant nothing to us.

We accepted the invitation and agreed to meet our new acquaintances at the camp. We reached the camp before dusk and easily found our hosts. They took us to an overcrowded, dirty room. More than twenty men, women, and children lived in the small room, which strongly smelled of sweat and urine. Two-tier plank beds and a metal stove in the corner were the only furniture in the area. There were many other such rooms in the camp.

---

[4] Literally "Men of Arms" in French. These Romanian militiamen were left behind by the Germans to police the area. They were armed gangs of young Romanians, who were not part of any military unit. They used force at will and answered to no higher authority.

Our hosts made a place for us to sleep at the foot of the plank beds and went to other rooms to collect some food for us. They came back with corn flour and started to prepare our dinner on the stove.

Word spread about the visitors who had come back from the dead. People stuffed themselves into the room to hear of our flight. German genocide in the Ukraine had been so complete that, after a year, very few Jews had returned alive from the German grasp. As soon as we stared to eat, the commandant burst into the room. He demanded that we leave immediately. He yelled that if the gendarmes found out that Jews from German territory were in the camp, all the residents would be in grave danger. Everyone in the room started to plead with him—"These poor men have not slept indoors for days and are exhausted. Where could they spend the night in such bitter cold?" Despite the pleas, he insisted that we leave. The people around us cried, "How can a God-fearing Jew set his own poor people out into the cold during the night?" The commandant finally agreed to let us stay for a few hours but warned us that we must leave when the moon sets in the morning. He said he would be back himself to make sure we had left. However, he did not come back, and we slept until sunrise. In the morning, we quietly started walking toward Kopaygorod.

We arrived in the city during the day, and the first thing that caught my eye was the sight of Jews walking the streets freely. We stopped the first Jew we saw and asked whether he knew where my aunt, Sonya Belinkaya, lived. He turned out to be a person deported from Bessarabia and told us to ask a local Jew. We finally found a local Jewish woman, and she told us that my aunt was not living in the city now. She did not know where my aunt went, but she told us where to find her parents-in-law. Neither my uncle nor I had ever met the parents of my uncle David. We barely knew Uncle David. However we hoped that his parents would know where Aunt Sonya and my grandmother were living now.

We came to their home, explained our situation, and asked for the whereabouts of my aunt Sonya and of my grandmother. They told me that my aunt and three of her sons now lived in Luchenets, with my grandmother. Aunt Sonya's eldest boy stayed with his paternal grandparents in Kopaygorod. Uncle David's parents had known my parents and received us well. They offered to feed us and allowed us to rest in their home. They lived in their own home with their daughter and son-in-law. Two other families, who were deported from Bessarabia, also lived with them. Despite this, they lived comfortably considering the times. They were bakers who sold bread and made a fair living.

Uncle Yankel still had some valuables and asked my relatives to help him sell them. Misha, the son-in-law, agreed to take him to the bazaar. This was doubly helpful, as there my uncle could also hire a ride to Luchenets, as merchants from the village came to the bazaar to trade. While my uncle was away, I learned more about life under Romanian rule. I, in turn, told them what had become of my family. My uncle soon returned with good news. He had arranged for a ride with a Gentile from Luchenets for the price of ten German marks. In addition the man had paid him fifty marks for his valuables.

In the evening, a horse carriage pulled up to the house, and the Gentile driver demanded that we pay him in advance. My uncle gave him the ten marks. Our relatives gave us a sack of peas to bring to Aunt Sonya. We thanked my relatives and departed. When we came to the first village, the Gentile said that his relative lived there and he wanted to stop there for an hour. We came to the yard, and the driver went into the house. After ten minutes he came back to the carriage and invited us inside. The house was very warm, and we took off our overcoats and sat down at the kitchen table. The man of the house left without saying anything to us and soon returned. His wife brought us bread, pickles, sauerkraut, and a bottle of moonshine. The man poured everyone drinks, which we drank with our food. We were hungry and ate everything on the table. After a few drinks of moonshine, I felt warm on the inside, and my head started spinning. As I became more intoxicated, the conversation in the house became distant. The host wanted to know who we were and where we were from. Shloyme told him that we were from Bessarabia and lived in the barracks and were going to Luchenets to visit relatives. Most likely they did not believe us and deduced our situation, but they asked about it no more. We wanted to leave as soon as possible both to avoid further questioning and to get to our destination. I—who was destined to meet the grandmother I had not seen for many years, and an aunt I barely remembered—wanted to get to Luchenets most of all. At the same time I dreaded having to answer why I ended up in these parts without my parents. What would I tell them about my family? Our driver finally said goodbye to his relatives, and we thanked them for the dinner and the warm reception and went out into the yard. The moon was now out. It had grown even colder outside. But we were no longer worried because we had only a two-hour ride to Luchenets left now.

When we climbed back into the carriage, we saw that the sack of peas was no longer there. We understood that the man of the house took it as payment for the food. That is why he went out into the yard. We did not protest because we wanted to leave as soon as possible. The carriage left the village, and we rode on a snowy, level, and moonlit field. We no longer feared the open moonlit place the way we did when we crossed the border. We felt safe. We had almost reached our destination when the driver said he had lost a snowshoe and had to return to find it. He told us we were only five kilometers from the village and should continue on foot. Once he finds the snowshoe, he will catch up to us and drive us the rest of the way. Yasha decided to stay with the driver because his frozen feet hurt from many days of abuse. We got out and started walking. It was bright as day, and the snow was packed close to the ground and easy to walk on. We moved fast to avoid freezing and soon arrived at the village. It was now after midnight, and there was not a single living soul outside. We were worried about Yasha and the Gentile. Perhaps this was not Luchenets but some other village? It seemed unlikely because there was no other road and there were no other villages in the vicinity.

The place was small, and we guessed that everyone knew everyone else. We decided to knock on any door and find out where my grandmother Menya lived. But no matter where we knocked, nobody opened the door for us. Finally someone told us that my grandmother's sister lived two houses away.

We knocked at the door for a long time before my great aunt answered. I explained who we were, but she did not understand. My grandaunt had never met me or my uncle and likely never knew of our existence. She could not understand how we ended up there in the middle of the night. She came outside, and we explained everything again and asked her to take us to my grandmother's house or to let us stay in her house for the night. She said we could not stay with her because her son had typhus and her house was already full of people. She said she would take us to my grandmother and asked us to wait outside while she dressed. After a few minutes she came back and led us down a moonlit square used for the bazaar. We were in the middle of the square when we saw three men walking toward us. Two of them were local Ukrainian policemen, and the third was Yasha. As it later turned out, the Gentile led him right to the police station, handed him over and told them about the other three Jews. The policemen knew my grandaunt and asked her who we were. She told them she was going to get the doctor because her son was feeling very bad, and we were neighbors escorting her, because she was afraid to be out alone. They told her she had nothing to fear and bade her to go to the doctor herself. They said they would hand us over to the Romanian gendarmes tomorrow and let them figure out who we were. My great aunt took off to my grandmother's house to tell her what had happened. The policemen told us to come with them. We were very frightened and felt bitter that we should walk so far just to run into policemen right here—at our final destination. If we ended up with the gendarmes, they would quickly find out who we are. If they do not kill us on the spot, they would certainly send us back to the Germans. And we had already counted ourselves saved. We had only walked a few paces when one of the policemen said, in Yiddish, "Give gelt!" (Give me money!) My uncle asked him how much he wanted. The price for freedom was ten marks. Uncle Yankel had only twenties and asked for change. The policemen laughed and told him to come to the station tomorrow morning to get his change. They let us go.

We saw the direction in which my grandaunt went and ran after her. The whole incident unfolded so quickly that she had not yet reached my grandmother's house. We entered my grandmother's house and stood in a small kitchen where a few people slept. We walked on to a small, kerosene lamp-lit room where more people slept. My grandmother sat motionless on her bed. Her eyes were hazy from sleep, and she did not recognize us. She could not understand why these dirty, ragged people stood in her dimly lit room in the middle of the night. I started weeping and threw myself at her, smothering her with hugs and kisses. "Grandmother, it's me, your grandson Moyshele; don't you recognize me? This is Uncle Yankel, and this is Shloyme Noodleman. You know them!" She finally understood and let out a scream. She shook, cried, and could not calm down. The woman who had opened the door for us also started kissing me and wailing. She turned out to be my aunt Sonya. My other relatives, including my step grandfather Gershshlieb and my mother's cousin Rosa, also embraced me. The noise woke up the rest of the people in the house. The children were scared of us and also started crying. After a while everyone settled down. I sat on the floor by my grandmother's bed and the others sat wherever they could find space. After regaining her composure, my grandmother asked me what had happened to my parents and other relatives. I told her that the Germans took me to camp in the summer, and I escaped. The others stayed in Kalyus, and I did not know their fate. I could not tell her the truth at that time. My relatives wanted to let us sleep in clean beds, but we asked to spend the night on the floor. My grandmother put clean sheets under the table and we fell asleep instantly.

We slept the remainder of the night and half of the next day. Neither the sound of the children's play nor the conversation of the adults disturbed our sleep. We were catching up on sleep for many months. While we slept, my grandmother went to her friends and relatives and got us some secondhand clothing. She also boiled a lot of water. When we awoke she made everyone leave the room and gave each one of us a bath. We helped one another wash off the dirt and lice that covered us from head to toe. We changed into the old, but clean, clothing and got haircuts from a barber, who was a relative of my grandmother. The barber also shaved Uncle Yankel, Yasha, and Shloyme. I was still too young to shave. After this, we started to resemble human beings again. We ate and fell asleep again. This was December 2nd, 1942—the seventh day of our escape from the camp.

Shloyme and Yasha parted ways with us the next day. They decided to pose as Ukrainians returning from a POW camp and find work at a nearby village. At that time, there was a shortage of working hands in the villages. Women, whose husbands were at war, gladly hired roaming laborers to help them in their fields and homes. Uncle Yankel stayed in Luchenets. He went to live with a woman he met there. I stayed with my grandmother.

As I said earlier, Luchenets was located in the Vinitskaya oblast of the Ukraine. When the Germans conquered the Ukraine at the beginning of the war, they handed the area between the Dniester and the Prud Rivers, an area referred to as Transnistria, to their Romanian allies. The Germans murdered all the Jews in the Nikolaevsky and Odessky region of Vinitskaya oblast, but did not have time to shoot the Jews in the rest of the oblast. The Jews who survived the initial German assault, the disease and overcrowding that followed lived on. The Romanians also exiled all the Jews of Bessarabia and Bukovina into the Vinitskaya oblast. These Jews were forced to walk a great distance to their final destination, and many were shot on the way or died of famine and disease.

The Romanians took this revenge on the Jews largely because of the latter's eager reception of the occupying Red Army in 1940. The Jews of Bessarabia greeted the Soviets with flowers and red ribbons because they believed the Soviets would end hundreds of years of harsh treatment of Jews. The Romanians promised vengeance for this act of treason. They kept their word.

Whereas the German brutal handling of the Jewish population was methodically planned, the Romanians had no plan at all. Former barracks, like the one where we spent the night, housed some Jews. However, the local Jewish population absorbed most of the unfortunate newcomers into their own homes. Many families lived in tiny houses, and there was terrible overcrowding. Infectious diseases spread quickly, and many died of typhus, dysentery, and other maladies. Others died of hunger, as there was not enough food to support the burgeoning populace. The transplants roamed from village to village and earned food with their trade. Those who were able to grab valuables before leaving their homes traded them for food. Those with neither a trade nor valuables begged for food. But the difficulty of their tasks increased because the Romanian gendarmes who saw Jews about the villages confiscated their food and beat them half to death—and sometimes to death.

I would spend a year and four months, from December 1942 to March 1944, in Transnistria. I still had much to bear until that time and had no confidence that I, or any of the Jews, would remain alive. The Romanians could decide to murder the Jews, as the Germans did, at any time. And the Germans themselves were a mere twenty-five kilometers away from us.

I spent the second part of the war in Luchenets with the relatives who adopted me. Luchenets was a small Jewish town where about nine hundred families had lived before the war. The Jews lived in the center of town, and the Ukrainian population lived around them, as was the custom in many Ukrainian towns where Jews resided. The majority of the Jews were craftsmen who serviced the local Ukrainian population. The remainder of the population worked at the collective farm. The Jews and the Ukrainians coexisted peacefully. The Jews lived in tiny old houses and were so poor they barely scraped together enough to buy food. My grandmother and her second husband Gershshlieb had lived there since 1938. My step grandfather was a tailor, and my grandmother was his helper. The Gentiles from surrounding villages all knew him to be good at his craft, and my grandparents lived more comfortably than most others. They lived in a small house that consisted of a bedroom and a kitchen. Right before the war, my grandfather's daughter Rosa came to visit with her infant boy. When the war started, they had nowhere to go. The child soon died.

My grandmother's daughter Sonya lived in the same house with her three sons—Aaron, Seyoma, and Yitzhak. Sonya's eldest son Misha stayed in Kopaygorod with his parents-in-law. Before the war, Sonya and her husband had also lived in Kopaygorod with four boys. Sonya's husband David was now fighting at the war front. When the Romanians came, they expelled part of the population to a camp, which they constructed in the middle of a field outside of Kopaygorod. Aunt Sonya and her boys were sent to this camp. By some miracle, she managed to escape from this camp with all her children. When she returned to her house, she found it occupied by Jews exiled from Bessarabia. They did not let her into the house. She turned to her parents-in-law for help and asked them to take her in. They took her eldest boy, who was seven, but refused to shelter the rest of the family. They bade her to go to her mother in Luchenets. Left with no means for survival, she and her children arrived in Luchenets, barefoot and barely clothed.

Three brothers, a bachelor, an elderly woman, and her son, all of them exiled from Chernovtsy, lived in the kitchen of my grandmother's house. A short time after I got there, the old woman died. Her son died shortly after her. Uncle Yankel and his woman took their place in our house. In all, thirteen people lived in a small room and a kitchen. This was typical of the crowded and unsanitary conditions that Jews endured in Romanian-occupied Transnistria. Infectious diseases commonly wiped out whole families. Romanians did not systematically shoot Jews, yet hundreds of thousands of Jews died from the cold, starvation, and disease (an estimated 270,000 Jews died in Fascist Romania).

This was my living condition after my escape from the German camp. Everyone in the house was always hungry. It was particularly difficult for my aunt Sonya to feed her three young children. Aaron was six years old, Seyoma was four, and Yitzhak was two. Our neighbors who dealt in contraband felt sorry for my aunt and shared their illicit goods with her. These illicit goods, which were considered contraband at the time, were matches, salt, and other household items. My aunt went to the bazaar with several kilograms of salt and sold it to the Gentiles out of a drinking glass. She bought flour, potatoes, and some beets with the pennies she earned. But this was far too little, and the children were always hungry. It was painful to look at these small, famished children— particularly for my grandmother. She always tried to sneak them some food, whether it was *mamaliga*, a piece of bread, or a cooked potato. Grandfather's daughter, Rosa, would scold her for it, but she paid no attention and skipped her own meals on many days.

But for me, the warmth and sympathy of my family and everyone else in the house more than compensated for my hunger. I was with my loved ones in relative safety, and, as far as I was concerned, that was enough.

My grandmother would often hug and kiss me while weeping. She no longer asked about my parents, brother, and sister. I think she already understood their fate at that time. The refugees in Luchenets who managed to save themselves from German-occupied villages told of the fate that had met the Jews there. But for the time my grandmother thought I did know of my family's fate, and we never spoke on the subject.

The winter of 1942–1943 was very cold and snowy. The rags in which I had arrived had worn out, and I had to toss them away. My clothes had been so worn and full of lice that, even at that time, it was impossible to look upon them without revulsion. My grandmother had found me a shirt and pants but could not procure a coat or shoes. My shoes had completely fallen apart, and I was forced to spend the entire winter indoors.

I spent many winter days with the three brothers, who were named Shulem, Herman, and Herbert. We often sat in the kitchen by the stove, and they tried to distract me from my misery. They were highly educated young men, having attended universities in Vienna and Bucharest. The brothers spoke French, German, Romanian, and Yiddish fluently. I found their company very interesting. They often spoke of their beloved native city—Chernovtsy. The three of them were born in this ancient, beautiful city in Transnistria, and they dreamed of returning to it.

I also became close to Aunt Sonya's boys. I felt bad for them because they wanted to play and constantly asked to go outside. But, they had neither warm clothing nor shoes, just the same as I. We lived like caged birds. By the end of the day, the kids would sit by the window waiting for their mother to return from the bazaar and bring them something to eat. They could not wait until the potatoes, beets, and *mamaliga* were cooked. They were so hungry that they sometimes grabbed the food and ate it raw. Thanks to the efforts of my relatives, especially my grandmother, I soon became myself again, both mentally and physically. However, I had a difficult time putting up with the inactivity. While nobody gave me a hard time about anything, I wanted to contribute to the household. All the adults were working so hard just to survive. They were always hungry, and every bowl of soup or piece of *mamaliga* they gave me, they took away from their own mouths. I could not wait for spring, when I would finally go to a town and find some work to help my relatives and myself. I also seethed with anger at the Germans, Romanians, and their local conspirators. I had been angry for a long time, but had used that anger to fuel my desire for escape. Escape was my revenge, and I had achieved it. But now I had no outlet for my anger because I had nowhere to go and nothing to do. I felt jealous of the soldiers and guerillas who bore arms against their enemies. I wanted to meet my tormentors on the battlefield on equal terms.

Finally the long awaited spring of 1943 arrived. The days got longer, and the sun felt warm once again. The heavy snows of winter started to melt, forming little streams that flowed into larger ones. The town became a large, impassable swamp. Despite this, everyone started to spend the days outside the house in order to feel the sun's warmth and breathe the fresh air after the long, difficult, and cold winter.

We heard that the Germans were defeated at Stalingrad [February 1–2, 1943] (today's Volgograd). Although Stalingrad was a few thousand kilometers from us, we were still very happy. We allowed ourselves a dim hope of liberation—if we could only stay alive a little longer. By that time, the swamp dried up, and it became warm and possible to walk barefoot. The spring was salvation for the children. They left the dirty, crowded house for the fresh air. They spent every day, from morning to evening, outside. My spirits also lifted as I ended my "house arrest" and thought I could finally occupy myself with something worthwhile. But it was not to be, because the Romanians had other ideas. With the start of spring came forced labor. The gendarmes took us to build a new headquarters—a gendarmerie and police station. They also made us load and unload railcars as well as repair the rails. The police barged into homes early in the morning and forced all the capable men and women to work. Very few were able to escape this backbreaking labor. On top of this, no amount of hard work could ensure that one would not be beaten. We were beaten by the Romanian gendarmes, the Ukrainian policemen, and even by some Jewish policemen who wanted to be favored by the Romanians.

Yet I was sometimes able to get away from the work and go to the Ukrainian village. There was always work in the village during the spring, but even more so now that most men were away fighting in the war. I would help landowners dig their gardens, plant potatoes, and do anything else required about the household. I worked from early in the morning to late at night. Unlike the gendarmes who gave us nothing in return for our work, the villagers fed me and sometimes gave me food to take home.

I worked very hard at the village, but at least it was voluntary labor with payment of food in return. I would sometimes stay overnight and sleep with the livestock. Some of the wealthier people in the village were rebuilding their homes or building new ones. They gladly took me in to help them. They fed me every day, and after a week's worth of work, would give me a few kilograms of corn flour as well as ten kilograms of potatoes to take home. I was happy with this meager salary. While helping build one of these houses, I dragged two water pails, held together by a heavy wooden plank across my back, from the water well to the house. This water was mixed with straw and other materials, and the mixture was dried in the sun to make bricks. This was difficult work, and I made hundreds of trips to the well each day. I was very thin, and the planks made my shoulders so raw that it was impossible to touch them without causing severe pain. However, I brought my meager earnings home and was happy to be of help to the family. And, also, I was fed, and having food was the most important thing at that time.

I was most afraid of meeting the gendarmes who occasionally appeared in the village, since they forbade us to leave the borders of the Jewish village—the ghetto. If I ran into them, I would get a merciless beating. The people I worked for sent their young children to keep watch on the street and let us know if the gendarmes appeared. If they did, I hid in the cellar.

Early one morning in the beginning of the summer, there was a forceful knock on the door. Three policemen burst inside and ordered Rosa, my grandfather's daughter, and me to get dressed. They took us to the police unit where a number of young men and women were already gathered. As the morning continued, the policemen brought more and more young men and women. Nobody knew what they were planning to do with us. My intuition told me that we were going to be transported somewhere distant, en masse. There was even a possibility we would be handed over to the Germans. I started to look for an opportunity to escape. There was none—the police guarded us closely. The family members of the detained waited outside the police building for some kind of news; the police offered no explanation. When the police were satisfied that they had gathered everyone, they told us that we were to be taken to Mogilev Podolsk and sent to work from there. They did not disclose the location or nature of the work. They then bade the relatives of the prisoners to bring clothing and food for the journey. I said goodbye to my family, never expecting to see them again.

In the afternoon, the guards arranged us into the now familiar column. We marched to Mogilev Podolsk under heavy guard consisting of Ukrainian policemen and Romanian mounted gendarmes. They herded us like sheep, shouting and lashing out with sticks and the butts of rifles, down a dusty road. We arrived at Mogilev Podolsk in the evening and headed to the railroad station. Two rail cars stood ready for us on the reserve rails. The guards locked us in the wagons from the outside. It was very crowded and only possible to sit down by pressing up tightly against one another. The railcar was hot and humid, making it very difficult to breathe. The only fresh air came in through a small barred window. After some time we were attached to a locomotive and started to move. None of us knew where we were going and could only guess. This was the first railroad ride of my life, and I believed it would be my last.

When we started moving, air started to circulate about the car, making it easier to breathe. I sat pressed against somebody's shoulder and could only think of the worst. I wanted to live very much and fought for my life with every ounce of strength I had. I had been near death many times, and some heavenly forces had saved me. Had my luck finally run out, or would there be another miracle? I needed to find a way out this situation and desperately searched my mind and surroundings for something to help me. There was nothing.

The train rolled into the night, taking us further and further into the unknown. Summer nights in the Ukraine are very short—dark comes late, and light early. But this night seemed endless to me. Still I must have napped for a short time because, suddenly we were no longer moving. I listened for the voices that were audible from the outside. By now everyone else in the car had awakened and was also listening for clues of where we were. The voices spoke Ukrainian, Romanian, and German tongues. We found out from bits of conversation that we were in Gmerinka, and that our cars had been unhitched and would soon be attached to another engine. I felt slightly reassured because Gmerinka was in Romanian-occupied territory. I knew that Romanians and Germans patrolled large railroad stations, and therefore the Germans' presence did not surprise me. I was hoping that they did not know of our presence. Everyone in the car was thinking the same thing and spoke to one another only in whispers that could not be heard outside the car. We soon heard the sound of an approaching train. It stopped, somebody attached our cars to it, and we were moving again.

As soon as the train was in motion, people started debating where we were going, and it got very noisy. One group was convinced we were heading north to the Germans. The other said we were going south to the Romanians. I did not take part in this debate and returned to thoughts of escape. At that time, the sun came up, and rays of light spilled into the car through the barred window. The sleepless night had ended, but the locomotive rolled on without stopping anywhere.

Everyone in the car grew quiet and nervously awaited the next day. Finally the train stopped in a small station. I felt our railcar separating from the train, which rolled on, and understood that we had arrived, and somebody would come for us shortly. Some anxious moments passed, and the door was finally unlocked from the outside and opened by a guard. He spoke Ukrainian, and ordered us to get out.

We helped one another climb out of the car and onto the railroad station, the name of which I have forgotten. I could barely stand after the sleepless night. It was now around noon, and the sky was a cloudless blue. The sun blinded me after the many hours spent in the gloomy darkness of the railcar. The guards brought me out of my daydream with their yells and sticks. I quickly noted that there were no Germans among the guards. They were Romanian gendarmes and Ukrainian policemen. I was relieved.

They arranged us in a column and marched us down a dusty road to a destination unknown. We walked fifteen kilometers to a village, which we later found out was called Dniestravarka, which was three kilometers from a town called Tulchin.

We arrived at a camp outside the village. Our barracks were inside a former horse stable. The guards marched both the men and the women into the stable. Two-tier plank beds lined the walls with a narrow passage leaving space to get around. Small, barred windows allowed minimal light to get into the stable.

The stable was dimly lit by kerosene lamps during the evening and night, and bats clung to the rafters. At night we were locked from the outside and if the straw caught fire from the lamps, we would surely have been burned to death. A short fence surrounded the camp, but the real escape deterrents were the Romanians and Ukrainians guarding us. The camp also had its own police made up of Bukovinian and Bessarabian Jews who could communicate with the Romanians in their native tongue. Some of these Jews were just as cruel as the Romanians and beat us with the same vigor as our jailers. I remember the last names of three of them even today. They had been policemen in the Mogilev Podolsk ghetto and were sent here by the Jewish administration as punishment for their cruelty. They were happy to come, because they could be even crueler in the camp.

There were roughly two thousand people in the camp. There were both local and Bessarabian Jews who lived in the villages in Vinitskaya oblast in the Romanian-occupied territory. So here I was, in a forced-labor camp again—this time in Tulchin under the Romanians. The work was easier, and the living conditions better than those in the German-run camp in Letichev. We were better fed, and death did not await us at every single step. The Romanians did, however, beat us just as much.

The Romanians erected the camp to supply labor for the construction of a power plant. A part of the prisoner population worked in Tulchin on the deconstruction of a large old synagogue. The

Romanians planned to build the electric station in its place using the materials from the original building. The building was to be taken apart very carefully in order to preserve bricks. A larger portion of the population, and the one I belonged to, worked on mining peat, a compacted deposit of decomposed organic debris to be used as fuel for the power plant, from a large swamp. The Romanians never got their electric station. The Red Army was conquering back territory quickly that summer, and the Romanians had things other than infrastructure projects on their minds. But they did manage to take apart the synagogue, brick by brick.

We were digging up the swamp using shovels, the most primitive method available. The work was exhausting. I spent all day barefoot in a ditch filled with foul-smelling swamp water, digging for the peat. I passed the peat up to women who carried it away on stretchers and laid it out to dry in the sun to make it usable as fuel. The skin on my feet became thin and clear from so much time spent standing in the water. After a while, the skin started to break and pop, and it became very painful to walk.

Each morning, the guards took us out of the stable at sunrise and assembled us into two columns. The camp's Romanian guards marched one group to the synagogue, and the other to the swamp. They watched over our work and beat us mercilessly for any infraction. We walked to work through the village and sometimes the Gentile women poured apples out of their buckets for us, as the guards did not allow them to hand anything to the Jews. We picked the apples up from the dusty road and ate them on the spot. Women stood in their gardens and looked at us with pity, wiping tears away from their eyes with their handkerchiefs.

We could only convey our gratitude by turning our eyes to them. I have to say that there were a lot of people in the Ukrainian population who showed kindness and understanding toward us and tried to help with whatever they could—especially on Romanian-occupied territories. This is likely because the Romanians did not punish Ukrainians who helped Jews as the Germans did.

A makeshift kitchen stood under an awning in one of the fields where we worked. During the lunch break, we received a bowl of soup, a piece of horsemeat, and a piece of *mamaliga*. I was sometimes able to get in line a second time and receive an extra portion of *mamaliga*. This was dangerous, for if the policemen saw a person do this, they would drag him out of line and beat him on the spot. When we returned from work in the evening, we again received a small piece of *mamaliga* and a cup of some drink that was neither tea nor coffee. This was my daily ration, which was scarcely enough to keep me from starving. Exhausted and demoralized, I would barely make it to my spot on the plank bed, eat my dinner, and fall asleep.

I spent two months doing difficult and exhausting work, which was accompanied by beatings and all sorts of other humiliations. During this time I devised many different escape plans but found it unrealistic to attempt any of them alone. I was looking for a partner and finally found the right young man. He slept in the same barrack as I did, and also worked in the peat swamp, but in a different work brigade. His name was Haim, and he was an eighteen-year-old Bessarabian. I do not remember his last name; or perhaps I never knew it—I did not concern myself with such trifles at the time.

Likewise I do not recall the features of his face. I only remember that he was of average height and was dark as a gypsy. Romanian soldiers had deported him and his parents from Bessarabia to Transnistria. The Romanians shot his father along the way, and he and his mother ended up in Luchenets. We became very close friends.

We were locked in the stable and left to ourselves at night. Anyone could do whatever he or she pleased under the dim lamplight. Some quietly rested on the hard beds after a difficult day of work, while others spoke in lowered voices about their prewar lives, their homes, and their relatives who were no longer alive. The women gathered in some corner on a plank bed. They had a lot to talk and cry about. It was doubly difficult for them because of the impossible physical labor and the threat of being raped by the guards. There were a few young women from Bessarabia who had fantastic voices and knew many Jewish songs. We often asked them to sing something for us. They would sit on the plank beds in the middle of the stable and perform songs that reflected the full pain and hopelessness of our situation and the bitter fate of our Jewish people. I listened to their songs as tears streamed down my face. I heard many of the Jewish songs for the first time. Some of them are still sung today like, for example, "Buy some cigarettes"—Kupite Papirosy, "Bagels"—Bubliki. Many of them are no longer sung and are completely forgotten. Likewise, my native Yiddish language is also disappearing.

Haim and I devised the following plan during the nights. Several ditches, dug before the war, now overgrown with vegetation, stood in the far corner of the camp. We decided to hide in these ditches before the guards took us back to the stable. Then we would wait until the guards went to sleep, climb over the fence and leave the camp. We warned our neighbors not to make any noise if we were not in our places on any given night. I asked Rosa, my stepaunt, to come with us. However, she was too afraid and chose to stay at the camp. All was ready, and we only waited for the right opportunity.

We got our break in the beginning of August. It was some Romanian holiday, and the guards told us to get into the stable earlier than usual. Before the end of the workday, Haim and I made a break for the ditches. We hid in separate ditches and lay still, confident that no one would find us there. Guards rarely went to that side of the camp and were even less likely to do so that day. They could not wait to start celebrating. The loud drunken voices of our guards were audible from the open windows of the house where they lived. We waited and waited, and their voices finally grew quiet long after midnight. We carefully climbed out of our ditches and assured ourselves that everyone was sleeping. We then quietly climbed over the fence and started running frantically. After running for some time and making sure that nobody was following, we stopped to catch our breath. We then started moving quickly, but pacing ourselves, to get as far away from the camp as possible before dawn. We planned to find some safe place, hide, and plan the next step. We walked on a deserted road with quick step. The night was quiet, warm, and cloudless. We were traveling light, as we had nothing with us except a bag with a piece of *mamaliga* saved from the previous night's dinner. We reached a village at sunrise but were afraid to enter it. Instead we found a cornfield that was removed from the road and lay down there.

The people of these villages usually rose very early, and the road was alive with movement shortly after sunrise. We now heard the barking of dogs because the Romanians, unlike the Germans, allowed villagers to keep them. This was a huge inconvenience to us because it was no longer possible to come up to a house without being noticed. The dogs started barking loudly when they sensed us, and all the other dogs on the street would echo them.

We ate our *mamaliga* and were in want of water, but there was none to drink. We did not dare go into the village at this time, but knew that we would have to go sooner or later. We needed food, water, and directions. When Haim and I planned our escape, we had only one thing in mind—how to get out of the camp. We did not even know in which direction to go, but we were convinced that if we made it to freedom, kind people would help us. We believed we could find food and get directions. We had achieved our first goal by escaping from the camp and getting reasonably far away from it successfully.

It was tranquil and comfortable to lie on the warm, soft ground among the corn stalks, and we soon fell asleep. We woke up because the sun was baking us, and we were tormented by thirst. It was afternoon, and the movement on the road had almost stopped as everyone was busy working in the fields or in their vegetable gardens. Haim and I decided to go into the village, come to the nearest house, and ask for water and something to eat.

We were an odd couple. Haim was a Bessarabian who spoke Ukrainian very poorly, and I had to do all the talking. However, my vision was very poor and he had to be the lookout. Haim's vision was sharp, and he could see danger from far away or, as it seemed to me, before it even appeared. His keen eye saved us from unpleasant meetings with police and gendarmes during our run.

We chose a house without a dog, came into the yard, and knocked on the door. Nobody answered. We went around the house and saw a middle-aged woman who was working in the vegetable garden. I called to her, and she asked us what we wanted. I asked for water and something to eat. Without uttering a word, she pointed to a well in the middle of the yard and went into the house. Meanwhile we lowered the wooden bucket that hung on a chain and pulled out fresh, cold water. We took turns gulping water and trying to quench our thirst. We only tore away from it to give each other a chance to drink and to draw a breath. We finally were satisfied, washed ourselves, and poured the remainder of the water onto the ground. By that time, the woman had returned with two jugs of buttermilk and two pieces of *mamaliga*. She motioned for us to sit at a homemade wooden table, which had been fixed into the ground under a tree. She poured us two cups of sour milk and told us to eat. The milk was cold, and the *mamaliga* was very tasty. We ate and drank insatiably and felt this was the food of kings, the likes of which we had never eaten. The woman did not ask us for anything, quietly watching us eat and pouring us more milk as we finished our cups.

We got very lucky—in our first meeting with a local person after our run from the camp, we ran into a person who treated us with sympathy and kindness. This simple Ukrainian woman gave us hope that there were good people in these lands—people who would not let us perish. Our hopes were not in vain. We met many good people who helped us get back to Luchenets. However, there were also many who drove us from their yards and set their dogs on us. We put a lot of trust in this kind woman. I told her that we escaped from a camp near Tulchin last night and were headed home to our village of Luchenets in the Kopaygorod region. I asked her how far we had gone from the camp, and in which direction we should travel to reach our destination. She answered that her village was twenty kilometers from Tulchin. She did not know where Luchenets or Kopaygorod was located. If they were in the same direction as Gmerinka, then we were headed the right way. Our plans did not include Gmerinka, which was a big railroad hub with a lot of Germans and Romanians. While Jews lived there too, ending up there was very dangerous, as we would be noticed right away. We decided to get directions along the way from someone else who knew the area better. The woman told us that there were no Jews living in the area, because the Germans had shot all of them before handing the territory over to the Romanians. She also told us that each village had leaders and police made up of local residents. While they treated their own people well, there was no way to know how they would treat us if they found us. It was clearly best to stay away from them. We expressed our deep gratitude to the kind woman. As a final act of humanity, she poured apples, pears, and plums into our sacks and wished us safe travels.

It was now long past noon, and the sun was at its hottest, and there were almost no locals outside. We decided not to tempt fate, which had been kind to us that day, but rather to leave the village and wait out the remainder of the day in a safe place. Disappearing from sight was not difficult in the summer. All we had to do was dig into the hay stacks that stood in the unharvested fields of corn, or hide in a ravine. Of course these places only worked if nobody was chasing us. Luckily nobody pursued us after our escape. We sat out the days in safe places and entered villages only when we needed food or directions.

We were traveling during the hottest part of the summer, and the heat was unbearable. It was difficult to find cover to protect ourselves all day. We also could not get anything to drink during the day and were dying of thirst. At some point later in our journey, an old man gave us a weathered military flask. We were then able to fill it at night and somewhat satisfy our thirst during the day.

After the unavoidable immobility and oppressive heat of the day, the cool night gave us strength and hope. We walked the deserted village roads while everyone slept. Our only greeting was the sound of barking dogs, which everyone ignored. Branches full of ripe fruit hung out from the edges of the yards and bent down to the road right above our heads. The overripened fruit lay at our feet in the dusty roads. We filled our sacks with the fruit and feasted on it in our daytime shelters. We ate mostly fruit and had to come into the villages only rarely during the day. As there were no Jews left alive in this region, our arrival would bring unwanted attention. When we came closer to houses, we picked carefully. We looked for houses that had large yards and could be approached without much risk. We tried to stay away from young people. We saw danger in every young man as he could turn out to be a policeman. People from the older generation, especially women, treated us with more sympathy than their younger counterparts. It was always the young people who would yell at us to leave and set their dogs on us.

We walked confidently at night because we knew we would not meet policemen or gendarmes. They preferred to serve during the daytime and slept through the night as calmly as the rest of the population. Nobody, except the Jews or those with loved ones at the war front, felt the effects of the bloody war that was happening. The Romanians treated the Ukrainians well, and the latter lived better than they had under the Soviets.

We heard rumors that the Red Army had defeated the Germans at Kursk. But Kursk was very far from us, and we still had little hope for a quick liberation. We were now getting closer and closer to our home. We took a roundabout path, trying to stay far from the railroad stations and places where police gendarmeries were located. We stayed on the move, never risking falling into the hands of the law. We wanted to get home to our relatives as soon as possible, even though we knew nothing good would be awaiting us there.

We finally got home late at night on the tenth day after our escape. My relatives, especially my little cousins, were thrilled to see me. Only my grandfather Gershshlieb was sad. He asked why his daughter Rosa had not returned with me. I told him that I had asked her, but she was afraid. I tried to calm him by telling him that she would return shortly. Luckily this really happened, and everyone had returned home by the beginning of October.

My return this time ended my camp imprisonment. Admittedly fleeing from Tulchin was far easier and less dangerous than escaping from Letichev. Still, we could not have known what the Romanians would have done with us if we stayed in the camp or got caught while escaping.

If I ever believed life would be easier upon returning, my illusions were dispelled instantly. The village was small, and the policemen quickly found out that I had returned. They forced me to do the most difficult work under threat of reporting my escape to the gendarmes. I could rarely escape to work in the village, and therefore could not earn even a little food for my labor. One day shortly after my return, I was working in the fruit and vegetable garden in the gendarmerie that was located in a former school. I was gathering fruits along with a group of young men and women. We packed boxes and baskets with fruit and took them to the basement. This work was relatively easy, and nobody watched me. It also allowed me to treat myself to an apple or a carrot, which was welcome, as I never got enough to eat.

When I finished my work, I wanted to take some apples to bring to my young cousins. Just as I began to stuff the apples inside my shirt, a gendarme stepped out to the porch. He saw what I was doing and called me to him. I let the apples fall to the ground and walked to him reluctantly. I knew he was going to beat me. By this time I had been beaten by Germans, Lithuanians, Romanians, Ukrainians, and even by Jewish policemen; but nobody had beaten me as badly as this Romanian gendarme. By the time the beating was over, I was bloody and just clinging to life. My fellow workers carried me home, and I lay in bed for two days. On the third day, the policemen forced me to go to work again despite my bruised face and body.

As I said earlier, I was forced to work for the Romanians much of the time. However, I maintained acquaintances in the Ukrainian village and sometimes I helped them around the house. There was an elderly couple, Vasily and Maria, who were particularly kind to me. If I came to them, they always fed me, even if they had no work for me to do. They also hid me whenever the need arose.

News spread that the Red Army had just liberated Kharkov. While the news gave us hope, our daily life did not get easier. In fact, the Romanians took revenge on us. They started rounding up young people and sending them away to work. I stayed alert and ran to the Ukrainian village for shelter. One time I almost got caught. The boys were playing outside, and they saw the policemen going from house to house grabbing young men. They ran inside the house and told me about it, but it was too late to leave unnoticed. My grandmother and aunt helped me dress into women's clothing and covered my head with a handkerchief. Then my grandmother and I ran to the house of Duvid Covel, the blacksmith and our neighbor. We passed right in front of the policemen. Duvid was the only blacksmith in the village and was considered untouchable by the authorities. His family was free from common work, and neither the gendarmes nor the policemen came into his house for searches. He worked in the collective farm's metal shop and did all the work needed by the authorities.

I hid in the cellar along with two other young men who managed to duck into Duvid's house. When the policemen came to my house, they asked where I was. My grandmother claimed to have no idea of my whereabouts. The policemen said they would take Aunt Sonya instead of me. When the children heard this, they started screaming and crying. Aunt Sonya took the younger in her arms, and the older grabbed her leg, and she insisted that she would take her children with her. The house rang out with noise and screaming, and the policemen relented. They left cursing and promising to find me anyway. I spent two days in the cellar before everything settled down, and I was able to return home.

It was the beginning of November, and cold rain was falling. The harvest had already been gathered from the village's vegetable gardens, and there was no more work for me to do. Winter was coming again, and I had no choice but to stay indoors. The Red Army had pushed the Germans back to the Ukraine and had retaken Kiev. There was now real hope of liberation. However, I was not sure I would live to see the day of emancipation, because I could not believe the Romanians and Germans would let the world hear the witnesses of their evil. My worst fears were confirmed when the gendarmes ordered all the men between sixteen and forty-five to appear in the bazaar square early one morning in December 1943. All who did not report would be given the strictest punishment. I had nowhere to hide, and Uncle Yankel and I joined all the other men. When everyone was gathered, the policemen took us to the gendarmerie.

The policemen told us we were being sent to work, but nobody believed this. There was no work to be done in late autumn. I thought that perhaps we would have to dig trenches. But if this were the case, we would be delivered to the Germans. The Germans would not leave us alive. I looked at my torn shoes and realized that I could not survive work in the cold autumn rains and the winter snows. If I did not die of a bullet, I would not survive the pneumonia I was sure I would catch. Either way, I could not survive. I shared my thoughts with Uncle Yankel, and we decided to run.

One of the Jewish policemen was an acquaintance. He was a twenty-two-year-old named Aaron. He had also managed to escape from the Germans, and his whole family had also been shot. He was a better person than the rest of the policemen, and I thought he might help us escape. At the minimum, he would not give us away for asking. I pleaded with him, but he declined to help us. He was afraid, but added that, if he happened to see us escaping, he would look the other way. The day was now ending, and Uncle and I decided to take the first chance to climb the fence. I figured that if we managed to make it over, we would head for the village and seek shelter with one of the sympathetic Ukrainian families.

We agreed that I would climb the fence first, and my uncle would cover for me. He was then to follow me to a prearranged meeting place, and we would run for the village together. Suddenly the moment came! Nobody was looking, and I dashed for the fence, quickly climbed over, and ran hard to our meeting point. My heart hammered at my chest as I waited for my uncle. I kept thinking somebody had been chasing me, but nobody appeared. My escape had been successful, and I started to calm down. I do not know how long I waited for my uncle, but it seemed a very long time to me. He did not show up. I could not wait for him any longer, because staying in one place was too dangerous. I turned to the village with a heavy heart. My uncle had survived the initial German assault in the army, escaped the mass shooting at Kalyus, and escaped Letichev with me. Was this his end? I believed I would never see my savior, my beloved uncle, again. He had laid down his life to save me.

I arrived at the village late at night. The cold and rain penetrated me to the bone. The village streets were deserted. I came to Vasily and Maria's house and knocked on their door. I told them I had escaped from the gendarmerie and asked them to hide me for a few days. I assured them nobody had seen me when I entered the village. They fed me and offered me to stay in the attic. They bade me not to come down until they called me.

The attic was full of straw. Vasily had also given me bags to use for covers. I dug into the hay but could not sleep. I kept thinking of my uncle. What could have happened to him? Was he caught while escaping? Perhaps he came to the appointed place and did not find me? He might be looking for me now, with no place to go. All kinds of thoughts came to me and kept me from sleeping. When I finally fell asleep, I had terrible nightmares—I was chased and caught by the Germans. I screamed and woke up in a cold sweat. It was quiet in the attic. The only sound I heard was the rustling of mice.

In the morning, Vasily brought me food and told me to lie there quietly and not let the neighbors find out about me. After three days of hiding me, my hosts decided to go to Luchenets and visit my family. They wanted to let them know that I was alive and to see whether it was safe for me to return. I asked them to find out from my relatives what had happened to Uncle Yankel. They soon returned, and Vasily climbed up to the attic. He told me that the gendarmes had sent everyone away, including my uncle, that night. Luchenets was quiet, and I would be able to return home in the evening. How could I thank these people? I wished them health and the safe return of their son, who had been serving in the army since 1939. God heard my prayer and rewarded their kindness. After the liberation, they came to us and shared their joy. They had received a letter from their son.

I returned home that night. My family knew I had escaped but had no idea where I was until Vasily and Maria came. Before the guards took the men away, they allowed the families to bring them food and clothing and to say goodbye. Uncle Yankel told my grandmother about our escape plans. Above all else, he wanted to save me. He waited too long after I went over because he wanted to give me the best chance at survival. Consequently his chance passed, and he marched out with everyone else. There was little hope he would return.

But in January of 1944, on a day when a nasty mix of snow and rain was falling, Uncle Yankel fell into the house. He was so weak he could not stand, and it was frightening to look at him. His bearded cheeks sunk deep into his face, and his eyes were hazy and lifeless. His clothes were shredded rags, caked with dirt and coal dust. His feet were wrapped with paper bags that were tied in place by ropes. He looked like a ghost from hell. We undressed him and found his body covered with bloody wounds. When I took the bags from his feet I found them covered in blood. We bathed him in warm water, taking great care not to cause him additional pain. I covered his wounds with some sort of ointment. He ate and drank warm water mixed with grass—the closest thing we had to tea—and fell asleep. When he awoke, he had a high fever and was completely unresponsive. He just stared at everyone with blank eyes. He did not know what was happening to him. Uncle spent a whole week in a half-conscious state. We called a doctor, but he threw up his hands. The patient needed medicine and nutrition; we had neither—we had to rely on God. But after a week, Uncle started giving us hope—his temperature dropped, and his wounds began to heal.

My uncle's girlfriend, Brana, who was a former nurse, put him back on his feet. She gave him extracts of herbs, covered his wounds with ointment, and attended to him until he was back to himself. He was finally able to tell me what had happened to him. First he told me what I already knew—he missed his chance to escape because he wanted to save me and was afraid to draw guards to him. That same night, the guards took the men to the railroad station, loaded them into freight cars, and sent them south to the city of Nikolayev. The Germans were building a bridge across the Bug River and were desperate to finish it as they were retreating from the oncoming onslaught of the Red Army. The prisoners lived at the foot of the bridge in unheated rail cars. The conditions were inhuman. The prisoners stood in knee-deep freezing water while working. Wounds from the work and the constant beatings covered Uncle Yankel's whole body. It was beyond the human body and spirit to survive these conditions, but somehow Uncle managed to board a passing freight train in the middle of the night. He traveled home by switching between freight cars. He slept on open platforms and unheated railcars, all the while suffering from exposure and hunger. He became very ill, his temperature rose, and his head was splitting with pain. It was a miracle that he survived; nobody else came back.

By the winter of 1944, the Red Army was storming through the Ukraine and freeing additional towns and villages daily. It was inching ever closer to us, and we counted down the kilometers and guessed at the hour of our liberation. My spirit rose, and every day brought good news. There were even rumors that partisans were staging guerrilla attacks on nearby forces. We neither saw them nor knew where the rumors came from, but we believed it all.

While the winter of 1944 was not as cold as the previous one, the snowfalls were just as frequent. The warmth melted the snow into a slushy mess, rendering the roads an impassable mixture of snow and dirt. It was difficult for the Red Army to advance in these conditions, but it was even more difficult for us to wait. We prayed for their arrival—faster, faster, brothers! Free us while some of us are still alive!

On the other hand, the weather also helped us. The Romanians stayed to their gendarmeries and appeared in our village a lot less. The policemen too stayed idle as they felt their end was near. There was only one persistent serious danger—the Germans. They were only twenty-five kilometers away. But they were no longer concerned with us either. Everyone knew that the end was near, but no one knew what sort of end it would be.

One day, the gendarmes heard that partisans had appeared in a neighboring village. They mounted their horses and galloped there. A firefight broke out and the head gendarme was killed. He was the cruelest one of the lot and had abused us at every opportunity. We were happy about his death but feared reprisal from the others, as the Jews were considered responsible for everything that happened everywhere. His comrades buried him in the middle of the town square. When the Soviet army came, they dug him up and threw him in the gutter. The Ukrainians quietly buried him in the cemetery.

We lived in a constant state of fear and listened to every sound during the night. We felt that the Romanians and Germans would come any minute to destroy our homes and murder us. Almost a month passed this way.

But one Friday morning at the end of March in the year 1944, the Romanians were no more around. They fled quietly during the night, and we were left without authorities. That same day, some sort of military unit entered the town. They were neither German nor Romanian. They wore uniforms we had not seen before and spoke Russian. At first I thought they were Red Army, but I was mistaken. They were Russians who served in the German army. They stormed our homes and demanded food and moonshine at gunpoint. We had neither. They raged all night, plundering anything of value and raping young women. Three of these cutthroats barged into our neighbors' house and put all the inhabitants against the wall. Two of them dragged two young women into the other room while the third held the rest of the people at gunpoint.

When the women started yelling and resisting in the bedroom, the chaos broke out in the other room. The soldier standing guard in the other room sprayed the room with his submachine gun, wounding a woman in the leg and a young man in the stomach. The young victim's name was Moyshele Zlotnik, and he was only sixteen, a year younger than I was, at that time. In the morning, a doctor came to attend to Moyshele but could not help him. There was neither medicine nor any equipment to operate on him. He died later that day, and was buried early Sunday morning. He died a painful five days before liberation.

A few hours later, the retreating Germans appeared. Since Luchenets was not near the main roads, these were not the main fighting units that were leaving with the heavy military equipment. The units were uncoordinated and were traveling on foot and horse carts, the only mode of transportation possible on the dirt roads around the town. These were not the happy and healthy Germans I had seen in 1941 in Kalyus. They were dirty, ragged, tired, and unshaven. They had sunken cheeks and eyes puffy from lack of sleep. They did not bother anyone, and we were even brave enough to come to their wagons. They asked us for the nearest Dniester crossing. I told them that the nearest major city was Mogilev Podolsk, but they answered that the Red Army had already taken it back. This news was ecstasy to us, because Mogilev Podolsk was only thirty kilometers away. But there were pessimists among us who said it was too early to celebrate. They believed that the SS would follow the retreating Germans and kill us.

Nobody slept during that or the next night. We all sat dressed and waited for the shooting to start. We were prepared for the worst. Finally shots rang out on Thursday morning. Everyone else rushed to the basement, but Uncle Yankel and I stayed upstairs and watched the Germans retreat. And then Uncle Yankel saw an avalanche of people clad in gray overcoats descending a hill from the side of the river. He jumped up and yelled "Moyshele! Look, ours, ours, ours are coming! We are saved!" We jumped on each other's necks and started crying. We ran to the basement to share our happiness. Everyone was screaming and crying with joy. The whole town, young and old, poured into the streets to meet our liberators. Even now, fifty years later, I cannot think of our liberation without feeling the anxiety and elation. Men, women, and children hugged the soldiers and kissed their faces. The soldiers, just boys themselves, smiled sheepishly and lifted children into their arms. They treated us to sugar and crackers. These unforgettable moments have stayed with me. I treat the veterans of the Great Patriotic War, as it has always been known in the Soviet Union, with great respect and gratitude. I see in each of them my liberator who saved me from certain death.

The initial units moved on continuing their pursuit of the Nazis. A new unit of Soviet soldiers moved into the town and stayed for a short time. The following morning there was a meeting, and everyone came. Among the speakers was a Jewish officer. He spoke emotionally of his family, which had been shot in Kiev in 1941. We were the first living Jews he met in the liberated territories and it made him very happy.

The villagers invited the soldiers to sleep in their homes. The women washed their laundry and mended their clothing. They slept in our houses and were given the beds while the residents slept on the floors. I remember one soldier who told me this was the first time during the war that he slept on a pillow and covered himself with a blanket. The soldiers were kind to us. I remember how they sat at our table and treated us in our house to a big loaf of bread, American canned pork, tea, and sugar. They felt sorry for us, especially for the frail and hungry children who huddled together while looking at the soldiers with both apprehension and curiosity. The solders took my cousins on their laps and spread a thick slice of canned pork on their bread and let them drink real, sweat tea—something they had not tasted during their short lives.

Military units kept coming and going. The soldiers fed us, and I started getting used to life without fear. For the first time I allowed myself to think about my future, rather than being preoccupied with my immediate survival. But this also made me feel the full impact of my loss. Yes, I had survived, but where are my parents, my little brother, and my sister? Why have they not lived to see this day? Only now my grandmother and I realized that we had no reason to conceal the truth about our family from each other. She knew everything from the start and had cried into her pillow every night. We now grieved openly together.

Shloyme came back to Luchenets to see whether my uncle and I wanted to go to Kalyus with him. Uncle Yankel agreed, but neither my grandmother nor Aunt Sonya would let me go. It was early spring, and there was still snow on the ground. I would have to walk over fifty kilometers in my torn shoes and ragged clothing. We agreed that I would go to Kalyus as soon the weather improved and the snow melted. Shloyme, Uncle Yankel, and Brana, now my uncle's wife, left early in the morning of the next day.

The ministry of war had now established offices in our area and was drafting all men between eighteen and forty-five. The workers of the ministry treated both the Jews, who had lived through all the horrors of occupation, and the Ukrainians as deserters. They took these inexperienced and untrained Jewish men, dressed them in military uniforms, and sent them to the most dangerous war zones. These men, who had survived the brutal occupation, died in their first battles. I was fortunate to be a year too young. I had to report to a military base to receive training in rifle and machine-gun use, marching, and military tactics.

Finally the warm spring days came, the ground dried up, and I turned my thoughts to my birthplace, Kalyus. I had not heard from Shloyme or Uncle Yankel since they left for Kalyus. My grandmother and Aunt Sonya tried to talk me into staying with them until the end of the war, but I insisted on leaving. I felt that if I did not return to Kalyus, I would die of grief. I had to go to the grave of my family and see it with my own eyes. Maybe somebody had survived and was waiting for me. I started to prepare for the journey. My aunt brought a bag that had held German sugar, and grandfather Gershshlieb sewed me a pair of pants from it. It was supposed to be a navy color but came out light blue instead. In addition to the pants I owned an old satin shirt and a pair of worn ankle boots. This was the sum of my earthly possessions.

In my last few days in Luchenets, I went to the bazaar early one morning. There was no real purpose for the trip, as I had no money and nothing to sell. I was just walking the rows and watching people haggle when a huge sergeant in full uniform asked me whether I wanted to buy a padded jacket. He opened his overcoat and showed me the new army jacket. I asked him how much he wanted, and he replied that he wanted not money, but three bottles of moonshine. Moonshine cost about ten rubles per bottle. While I did not have money, I had a way to get the moonshine. I asked the sergeant to wait, and I ran to Mort-he Tswonbenkel's house. Mort-he was a distant relative of mine who secretly made and sold moonshine. I really needed a jacket and asked my relative to sell me the moonshine on credit. He did not deny me and asked only that I bring back the bottles at once. He told me not to worry about the money and to pay him back when I had some.

I quickly ran back to the bazaar worrying that somebody would get ahead of me. I found the sergeant, and we filled his flask with the moonshine. I was so happy that I would finally have some warm clothing. He started to unbutton his overcoat and then the padded jacket. I glimpsed a chest full of medals and suddenly heard him say, "You son of a bitch, German accomplice . . . !" He continued, "I am a Hero of the Soviet Union, I spilled blood for you; and you want to undress the Red Army; you will go in front of the tribunal. Get out of here!" I do not know whether he really was a Hero of the Soviet Union, the recipient of one of the highest medals awarded; I started crying both from frustration and from fear and left him. He went back to the bazaar looking for more victims. When I calmed down I came to him again and asked him to pay for the moonshine. He cursed and said, "Get out of here, you bastard; don't interfere with my work, or I will shoot you like a dog." After surviving years of occupation, I would not risk my life at the hands of a countryman. I walked back to Mort-he's and gave back the bottles. My debt was forgiven. I still had no jacket.

Finally the day of my departure for Kalyus came. It was the middle of May 1944, it was warm and nobody could stop me. My grandmother and my aunt Sonya were still trying to talk me out of going. It was difficult for them to let me go, because they knew what waited for me there. But their crying and arguing could not stop me. I was steadfast in my decision, because I was drawn to my paternal home: the place where my childhood was torn apart, where my family, friends, and a whole Jewish village lay in a mass grave. I hoped for some miracle, and nothing could hold me back. I had to see everything with my own eyes.

In the morning, I said goodbye to my family. We all spilled a lot of tears. My grandmother gave me half a loaf of bread and a few hard-boiled eggs, and I left. I planned to walk to Kurilovitz, the halfway point between Luchenets and Kalyus. I hoped to spend the night with Idle Bobic, an acquaintance from Luchenets. He escaped the firing squad in Kurilovitz as all the other Jews were murdered.

I arrived in Kurilovitz in the evening. I had never been there and had no idea how exactly it had looked before the war. I knew that it was a beautiful Jewish town where many Jews had lived. It had been known for its vibrant young Jewish population. But now, instead of Jewish homes, there were vacant lots filled with either ruins or vegetable gardens. A tiny number of Jewish homes stood intact, but Jews no longer lived in them. Only a few Jews who escaped the firing squads by some miracle returned to the ruins of their town.

While looking for Idle, I met a young woman named Manya Fradis. Just like me, she had escaped Letichev and lived in Luchenets. She was six years older than I was. I had not known her in Letichev, but we got to know each other in Luchenets. Manya was surprised to see me and inquired what I was doing there. I explained that I was going home to Kalyus and was now looking for my acquaintance in order to spend the night. She invited me to spend the night in her place. She lived in her grandmother's former home. I gladly accepted, and we walked back together.

We entered a small room furnished with a table, a few chairs, an old couch, and a metal hospital cot. There was no furniture in the other rooms, and the rest of the house was empty. I washed up while Manya made dinner and tea. As we dined, an oppressive silence spilled into the room. There was neither the sound of children playing outside nor the laughter of teenagers going out. Outside our window it was as silent as in a cemetery. We sat together on the couch in the moonlit room like two ghosts returned from another world. All the pain, anguish, and suffering that had filled us in the last few years came pouring out. The wounds in our souls could not stop bleeding, and everything we had experienced was tearing us to pieces. We talked of our wanderings during these difficult and frightening years. We spoke of our loved ones and friends who no longer lived. We cried like little children without anyone to console us. Dead silence surrounded and engulfed us. There was no living soul around.

Manya was disenchanted with her return home. She found nothing but ruins. The Gentile population, that was a minority of Kurilovitz before the war, now made up its entire population. They did not care for Jews who had witnessed their cooperation with the German genocide. For them, the Jews were too much trouble, and it would be much better if they were not around. In a day or two, I would face this attitude too in Kalyus, but for me it was no longer unexpected. Manya told me she could not remain here and would find another place for herself. She advised me not to remain in Kalyus. Building our lives on the ruins of a former existence would be impossible. May nights are very short, and it was dawn before we knew it. We were two torn souls with fates that were very similar. We shared our pain and suffering with each other and felt a little better.

We said goodbye in the morning, and I left for Kalyus. We agreed to meet again soon, but she left Kurilovitz, and we did not meet again until the beginning of 1945 in Mogilev Podolsk.

On the road to Kalyus I met a first lieutenant who was walking to Rudcavtse, a village only two kilometers from Kalyus. As we walked together, he told me that he had been wounded and recently discharged from the hospital. The military allowed him a two-week leave. His family was alive and unharmed and was eager to see him. We walked toward our respective birthplaces, the places where our childhoods had passed. His family, neighbors, and friends were all there to meet him. How I envied him! A mass grave and a village that no longer existed waited for me. This is what it meant to be a Jew in the Ukraine in 1944. We stopped in the village of Kalutze Berbovitch on the way home. He had some friends who lived there. It was Sunday, and middle-aged men and women sat at the table in the house we entered. They ate, drank, sang, and had a good time as if there had been no war and had never been an occupation. Nothing at all had changed in their lives. They made a place for me at the table. We ate and drank quickly and went on our way. My travel companion was in a hurry to see his family. For me, it was the opposite: my heart grew heavier with each step in the direction of Kalyus, and my legs began to fail me.

Kalyus could be entered on two different ways: one was via a mountain path which passed the old Jewish cemetery, crossed the bridge over the river, and led right into the middle of the village. This is the path that was used by the merchants coming in and out of the Kalyus bazaar. Kalyus could be seen unfolding as if in the palm of one's hand from this path. The other path was along the railroad tracks that also cut across the mountain and snaked past the mill. This was the road which cars and horse carts used when they traveled to Novaya Ushitsa or Kurilovitz. I chose the second path because it was the longer one. I now dreaded a meeting with my old village and stretched out the hour before the reunion. I knew that I would find nobody there, save for Uncle Yankel and Shloyme, if they had not been drafted. When I came to the outskirts of the village, my legs buckled and my heart hammered at my chest. I tried to regain my composure and sat on a rock at the side of the road and closed my eyes. My thoughts took me back to the events during my two-year absence.

Exactly two years ago, at the end of May 1942, I walked this road toward Novaya Ushitsa and then slaved in the forced-labor camp in Letichev with a group of other men and women. We had hopped to return in a month or two to our family. But I was coming back alone, two years later, and would not find any family alive. Three months after we had left, the Germans walked them down this very road for their last journey. They believed the ghetto had been closed and that they were going to Novaya Ushitsa. They believed this for some time, but when the Nazis turned the column toward the Dniester River, they all understood their fate. I could mentally see my family and friends on this death march and began to cry inconsolably. I sat on that rock for a very long time. When the sun began to set, I got up, wiped away my tears, and walked—back onto native ground.

Kalyus, like Kurilovitz and hundreds of other Jewish villages across the Ukraine, no longer existed. Vegetable gardens and a few undamaged houses were all that remained in place of the once vibrant village. I later found out that the Germans sold Jewish homes for kopecks (pennies) to the Ukrainians in surrounding villages. The latter took them apart for wood to be used in their fireplaces. Gentiles from the Ukrainian side of the village also bought some of the Jewish homes and now lived in them. They made themselves vegetable gardens on the sites of the deconstructed homes. It was so painful to see this. I had known every person who had lived in every home.

My home was one of the undamaged ones. I came to it with the heaviest of hearts and knocked on the door. Brana opened the door for me. Nothing had changed inside the house. Everything was exactly as it had been two years ago—everything, except my family.

Brana told me that my uncle and Shloyme had been drafted, and that she lived with my mother's friend and distant relative Rahil Bader. Amazingly Rahil saved herself from the firing squad and had been hiding with Ukrainians in the village of Kurazhin. She passed from house to house, from one family to the next. She had spent two years lying in basements and attics and had not seen the light of day during that time. She only moved between hiding places at night and during foul weather. She could only breathe fresh air in the dead of night. The families risked their lives for her. Our meeting was very emotional. We had so much to tell each other and spilled more tears. She did not have any children of her own and poured all her love and support into me. Brana had never treated me well, but Rahil kept me from feeling lonely.

The next day Rahil and I walked to the mass grave where our family was shot and buried. A government committee had been at the gravesite to investigate and document the atrocities of the German occupiers. This committee had established that eight hundred and fifty citizens, of the Jewish nationality, from the village Kalyus had been shot here[5].

Thirty years later, in the mid 1970s, I asked the Novaya Ushitsa planning commission for permission to erect a monument at the mass gravesite of the Jewish population of Kalyus. I offered to do it at my own expense. My request was denied. The head of the commission told me that he had no documents to confirm the deaths and could not grant me permission to mark the site. When I reminded him of the commission for German atrocities he told me to apply to a higher official in the

---

[5] As noted earlier, the commission found 540 bodies in the mass grave. The documents were sealed from the public and my grandfather did not know their contents when he recorded this memoir. The report omitted the "Jewish Nationality" of this victims

Soviet ministry and not to him. In 1978, without permission, I erected a monument despite the personal risk. I was ready for all sorts of trouble. Thank God, no trouble ever came of it, and the monument stands there to this day. [Moyshe had to lead an excavation and relocation of the gravesite, to a nearby location, in the early 1980s, due to construction of the reservoir. I led a small group of relatives to the gravesite every year on August 20th. We paid tribute to our family and friends on this saddest of days. Every one of the survivors thanked me for erecting the headstone. When I found out about the planned reservoir I had to erect a new monument and move the remains of the villagers and my loved ones. Seeing bulldozers and moving remains, and bones on the dirt roads opened up old wounds. Unfortunately there is nobody left to go there now—nobody to look after the gravestone.

But for now let's turn back to 1944. When I planned to come to Kalyus I did not think about what I would do there or how I would support myself. I hoped to find my uncle and seek his help. With my uncle away, I turned to the Ukrainian planning office for help. They offered me a job as a horse coachman at the collective farm. Later I found a temporary job packing fruit for a Novaya Ushitsa factory with a field office in Kalyus.

One day, the postman handed me a stack of letters, from relatives of Jews who had lived in Kalyus—the stream of letters continued for some time. They wanted to know the fate of their relatives. The local authorities asked me to respond to these letters because I knew everyone who had lived in the village before the war. What could I tell these people? There were only two possible answers: "Shot in Kalyus on

August 20th, 1942," or "Shot in Letichev in 1942 or 1943." Everyone had met the exact same fate.

There was also a letter from Aunt Sima, my father's sister who had lived in Mogilev Podolsk before the war. I had had no idea what had happened to her during the war. She had evacuated Mogilev at the beginning of the war and was now living in Udmurtia, a distant Ural region of Russia, with her three children. Her husband went to war, and she knew nothing of his fate. In her letter she asked me whether anyone had survived. I answered her that my uncle and I were the only survivors from our large family. We exchanged several letters, and she said she would take me into her home as soon as they returned to Mogilev Podolsk. She kept her promise. But that was later. For now I continued to live in Kalyus.

Two Jewish army officers, who had once lived in Kalyus, came back to Kalyus. Their names were Abrasha Katz and Aba Kramer. Their families had died with the rest. They came in a military car and stopped over at Victor Kulchitsky's. I came to meet them at Victor's and found them eating lunch with a sergeant and a soldier who was their driver. They invited me to sit down. Katz and Kramer, who were my parents' age, did not remember me but had known my parents well. After lunch they asked me to take them to the mass grave. The trip to the gravesite and the moonshine they had drunk made them feel sorry for me. They were saddened by my ragged appearance. I was still wearing the German sugar-bag pants and a shirt of indeterminate color. They promised to send me a military uniform. But as soon as they left Kalyus, they forgot about their promise. They forgot about the existence of a thin, unfortunate orphan who lived in Kalyus and really needed their help. Many years later I met Katz under different circumstances, as a man of equal footing. I asked him whether he remembered a boy he met in Kalyus in 1944 at Victor Kulchitsky's. I asked him whether he remembered his unfulfilled promise to send me a military uniform. He grew ashamed and made excuses, but by that time I did not need his excuses.

But there were also people who treated me with kindness and understanding. In the summer of 1944, I was almost seventeen. The war was still in progress, and I had to report to the Ministry of War for the draft. The ministry wanted to determine whether I was fit for military service and asked me to appear before the medical commission. My vision was already poor, but there was no eye doctor in Novaya Ushitsa, and I had to go to Kamenets Podolsk. I arrived there at the end of the day, and the clinic was already closed. I decided to spend the night with a Jewish family, a mother and a daughter who just returned from evacuation. They were nice enough to take me in but had no place other than the floor for me to sleep. We had dinner, and I told them my story. They advised me to go to a neighboring home where injured veterans gathered. They were the unfortunate Jews who returned from the war to find out that their families had been murdered. The gatherings were intended to provide support and company; the women thought I might find some comfort there. I entered the house and saw ten disabled men talking among themselves. They were all interested in the newcomer and asked me to tell them my story. After I finished, a man in his forties, who was missing an arm, came to me and said: "Listen, young man. I had a family. I had a son like you. They were all killed. Stay here, we will live together. I will replace your father, and you will replace my son. I will find you work, and, when the war ends, I will send you to study. Stay, you will not regret it. What is there for you to do in Kalyus? You will perish there." I cannot say why I refused him. It may have been pure frivolity. I do not remember the man's name, but I am very thankful to him for his kindness and sympathy for me.

The medical commission declared me unfit for military service because of my poor vision, and I returned to Kalyus. A surprise waited for me at home. Uncle Yankel, who had been wounded in the leg and moving from one hospital to another, came home for a few days. We had not seen each other for six months and were very happy to meet again. My uncle asked me to stay in Kalyus until the end of the war. If he managed to survive the war, he wanted us to live there together. He left me his overcoat and tried to give me the rest of his uniform. However, he could not return to the hospital wearing only his underwear. I also received a letter from Shloyme who was in the army which was steadily advancing toward Berlin. In the spring of 1945, he sent me two packages from Germany with clothing to fit me from head to toe. Thanks to him I had clothes for a few years.

Shortly afterwards, Aunt Sima returned to Mogilev Podolsk and asked me to come live with her. In the fall my temporary employment in Kalyus was ending, and I did not want to spend the winter in Kalyus. I left Kalyus on foot in the same clothing I had worn when I came in.

I once wanted to come to Kalyus with all my soul. But now I wanted to leave it just as much. It was difficult for me to walk the empty streets that were overgrown with grass, difficult to look at vegetable gardens where Jewish homes once stood. The voices of the people who had lived in those homes haunted me. Scraps of memories of my old life always resurfaced:

I could clearly remember when I was five years old, and my grandfather took me with him to synagogue. I stood among the praying Jews, and many would come over and pinch my cheeks, delighted at such a little boy coming to services. I really loved going to synagogue with my grandfather. On the way to the synagogue, my grandfather held me by the hand and told me religious stories, which completely captivated me. After synagogue, my grandmother fed us; she would make tzimis from beans, sweet cake from corn meal, and hot tea that she poured out of a large lead teapot. There was always hot tea in this teapot, after the bread was baked on Friday evening, and it remained on the warmer all of Saturday, as my grandparents faithfully observed the Sabbath and did not engage in any work on the holy day.

In 1934, my sister Ronya was born, and I started school. My parents sent me to the Jewish school, and I studied there for six years. I am very grateful to them, because I learned Yiddish there and still consider it my native language. My parents worked from a very early age and never had the opportunity to study. They were illiterate and could not prepare me for school in the way parents do today. In great contrast to the many children today, who can read, write and count by the time they reach school age, I came to first grade without knowing a single letter. I was a quick learner and moved to the head of the class quickly. I finished first grade on the honor roll and stayed there every semester of my schooling. I fell in love with literature and started to read everything I could find. I almost read the entire school library. During the long winter nights, I read to my family by the light of the kerosene lamp. They heard the bittersweet stories of Sholem Aleichem, Mendele Mokher Sefarim, and other great Yiddish writers. Mathematics also became my passion, and I often took first place in the school's academic Olympiad.

I remember my first teacher, Anna Abramovna. She was a tall, beautiful young lady whom the class nicknamed "the doll." She was also a terrific teacher who did not confine her lessons to the classroom. She often took us to the forest for our botany lessons. We collected lilac, which bloomed beautifully in April, and returned very happy, carrying large bouquets.

I had many friends that I knew my whole life, who went with me to the Jewish and, later, Ukrainian school. Their names were Misha Bronstien, Misha Koifman, Aaron Fleisher, the Fleishman brothers, Lyova Friman, Fleika Presavata, Brushale Katz, and many of my kin— the Rekhtmans. Unfortunately, there are also many I do not remember. They were kind, smart, and talented kids. They were good students; some of them played musical instruments and played in the school orchestra. They went to Olympiads in the regional center. Some of them were sure to become famous musicians or composers. But their abilities were destined to die at the earliest stage of their development. Not one of my school friends, or any of the other Jewish children of Kalyus, survived the Germans in 1942.

My family celebrated religious holidays together at my grandparents' house. I fondly recall one particular Passover celebration.

A large table now dominated one of their two small rooms. My grandmother crammed the table with a variety of foods and many candles, which lit the room beautifully. Grandfather, dressed in his talis (prayer shawl), sat at the head of the table and cast a warm, loving glance at his large family. My father sat on grandfather's right with my mother and his three children. My uncle Yankel, his wife, and three children sat on grandfather's left, opposite us. The men recited the Passover prayers in unison, covering the miracle of the Hebrews' exodus from their bondage in Egypt and their ascension to their holy land of Israel. As the youngest child who knew how to read, I had the honor of asking my grandfather the four questions (Ma Nishtana). These are the four questions that children ask their fathers or grandfathers on the first and the second night of Passover in order to appreciate fully the blessings of freedom. Our grandmother fussed over her children, constantly peppering us with kisses and loading our plates with food. The ceremony continued late into the night, and the youngest children began to doze right at the dinner table. They were whisked into the other room, and the ceremony continued. My own eyelids felt heavy, and my eyes began to close, but this was too interesting for me, and I fought off sleep with all the willpower I could muster to see this celebratory dinner to its end. I did stay awake until the end, feeling spent but joyous and fortunate. My grandparents, as Orthodox Jews, followed the laws of Judaism faithfully, and instilled these covenantal obligations into their children and grandchildren. Everything that I have in me that is Jewish was put there by them. I loved my grandparents dearly, and their memory will forever remain in my heart.

My memories tormented me because everyone in these memories lay in the mass grave by the river. The Ukrainians treated me with sympathy and kindness, but I could not find friends among them. The local authorities treated me with disdain. To them, I was an eyesore and an unpleasant reminder of their inaction. I regretted turning down the veteran's offer at Kamenets Podolsk, but it was too late to find him.

I left Kalyus and never returned to live there, but while living in the Ukraine I never failed to go to Kalyus on the grim anniversary. I came to the gravesite but never crossed the threshold of my childhood home again. Aunt Sima took me into her home and treated me as if I were her biological son. This was despite her poverty-stricken lifestyle and difficulty feeding her own three sons. I lived with them until a few months after the war ended in May 1945. I left in October, when I married my wife Shura and moved to Chernovtsy, where we spent the next forty years until our move to America.

This ends the story of the most difficult part of my life. But I must say a little more about a few of the people who made up this history.

Uncle Yankel could not find peace after the war. He lived in Kalyus, his ancestral home, for another fifteen years. He and Rahil were the only original Kalyus Jews remaining there. Uncle Yankel worked as a tailor for the Gentiles, as his parents had done before him. He left his second wife and married a third woman. His marriages were unhappy, and he always remembered that his true love and three children were buried just a short walk from his home. His difficult life before and during the war took a heavy toll on his health as well. He suffered from many ailments and became diabetic. The seemingly immortal Uncle Yankel, who survived some of the Second World War's bloodiest battles and escaped from two death camps, all the while keeping me alive, died in 1968. He was only 55. He did, however, have a daughter with his third wife. My cousin Mila lives in Israel with her family to this day.

Shloyme Noodleman and I stayed in close contact despite living hundreds of kilometers apart. His daughter Basya lived with us for four years in the 1960s while attending the University in Chernovtsy. Shloyme and his family immigrated to Israel in 1993. A short time later, he died. He was in his eighties. Basya still lives in Israel with her family.

I never saw Yasha again. He was most likely drafted into the army after the liberation and died in the Red Army's march to Berlin. I tried to find him after the war but could not. If he had survived, I would have been able to locate him, or somebody would have known of his whereabouts.

Haim, my fellow escapee from the camp at Tulchin, contracted typhus two months before we were liberated by the Red Army, and he died. His mother came to terms with the death of her husband but could not bear the death of her only child. She died soon after him.

Anna Abramovna, my first teacher, gave birth to a little girl right before the war. The Germans gunned her down clutching her child in her arms. Many years later, I had the chance to meet with her sister while working at a store in Brooklyn, New York. She was also an immigrant from the Soviet Union. When she heard I was from Kalyus, she wanted to know whether I had ever met a young teacher named Anna. It was only then, so many years later, that she learned the fate of her sister. We talked for a long time, and she promised to bring me pictures of her lost sister and my favorite teacher. I had many more teachers, but it is the young, beautiful, and intelligent Anna Abramovna that I always remember. I was eager to catch one more glimpse of "the doll," but it was not to be. Her sister never came back and I never saw her again.

The three brothers Shulem, Herman, and Herbert who lived with my family in Luchenets, all survived the war and returned to Chernovtsy. We became close friends, and we often spent time together. Two of them, Shulem and Herman, later moved to Romania, and from there to Israel. Herbert died tragically in Chernovtsy when he was accidentally electrocuted in the factory where he worked.

Manya Fradis, the woman in whose house I spent a night in Kurilovitz, and I met each other again at the end of 1945 in Chernovtsy. She later married a Polish Jew who was crippled in the war. She left with him to Poland. Before she left, I came to say goodbye. The third time we met was forty years later in 1985, in Vienna. I was on my way to America. I happened to have their phone number and called them. The old couple came to the hotel. We didn't recognize each other at first. So much time had passed; but we still remembered each other. We spoke little of the past. Her husband warned me that her mind had grown unsteady with age, and it was best to leave the past behind.

Shura and I have two terrific daughters, an amazing granddaughter, and two wonderful grandsons, as well as three sweet great-granddaughters[6]. I was destined to survive to start this blessed family. Thank the Almighty.

---

[6] To his delight, Moyshe Rekhtman's family has continued to grow. As I prepare this book for publication in 2008, he has six great-grandchildren.

www.ingramcontent.com/pod-product-compliance
Lightning Source LLC
Chambersburg PA
CBHW030758150426
42813CB00068B/3242/J